GOLF GURUS

The Wisdom of the Game's Greatest Instructors

James Bartlett

TAYLOR
Publishing Company

Dallas, Texas

Published by Taylor Publishing Company
1550 West Mockingbird Lane
Dallas, Texas 75235

Library of Congress Cataloging-in-Publication Data

Bartlett, James Y.
       Golf gurus : the wisdom of the game's greatest instructors / James
          Barlett.
       p.   cm.
       ISBN 0-87833-912-4
       1. Golf—Study and teaching.   2. Golfers.   I. Title.
      GV962.5.B37   1996
      796.352'07—dc20

Printed in the United States of America

10 9 8 7 6 5 4 3 2 1

CONTENTS

INTRODUCTION

In 1992, a somewhat obscure golf professional from Austin, Texas, published a book that was largely idle scribblings and notes from his long career teaching mostly country club hackers and one or two fine players. The golf pro was, of course, the late Harvey Penick, and the book was *Harvey Penick's Little Red Book*.

Harvey's little book, filled with his gentle humor and his deep wisdom about both golf and life, struck a major chord with the golfing public. It instantly became a bestseller, and one of the top-selling sports books of all time.

Penick's book, unlike the hundreds of other golf instructional volumes that crowd golfer's bookshelves, devotes few pages to the mechanics of the swing. In fact, distilled, the *Little Red Book* has but one memorable piece of advice for golfers: "Take dead aim." But Penick's book is peppered with notations on how to practice, how to prepare to play, and how to enjoy the game. It also offers vignettes—parables, even—about people Penick had known and instructed over the years. In this sense, Harvey Penick was a true Teacher, in the capital "T" sense, which is the true definition of a "guru": a personal religious teacher and spiritual guide. On the surface, the *Little Red Book* (and the *Little Green Book* that followed) is about the game of golf. In fact it is about the game of life.

It was in that spirit that I selected the teaching professionals profiled in this book. They are certainly not the only golf gurus in the world today, and this book should not be construed as an attempt to rate them as the best gurus. Rather, I selected these teachers because they all have something to teach that extends beyond the game. They came from different places and different times, their careers evolved in different ways, they worked to pass on different ideas about golf. But in the end, they are teachers, and some may even be Teachers.

There is an old bromide in the golf business that says "Those who can't play, teach." Like most old bromides, this one is oversimplified and tends toward gross generalization. Although true that many of these gurus failed in their attempts to play professionally on the tour, it does not follow that they would become "gurus" as a result.

The best teachers are those who know how to communicate, whether teaching quantum physics or the mysteries of the sand shot. The gurus profiled here who work with Tour clients believe that because "they have been there"—in the cauldron of competitive tournament golf—they can communicate more effectively with their pupils. But the 26-handicapper struggling to control his chronic slice couldn't care less about the sensation of trying to hold a two-shot lead down the stretch in an important tournament. And our gurus know that as well.

All of them admit that although it is gratifying, intoxicating, and remunerative to work with the world's best golfers, they derive more personal satsifaction from helping that 26-handicapper learn how to hit a draw. That is why they became golf instructors in the first place.

In any case, as mentioned, this book does not provide an exhaustive list of the world's golf gurus: there are dozens of other fine teachers doing stellar work and helping the games of top players, and I'm certain their stories are worth retelling. Maybe work should begin shortly on "Golf Gurus II!"

I'm endlessly amazed at how few golfers realize the efficacy of employing a regular teacher and taking frequent lessons. You will read about some of the "students" and "pupils" of the gurus: they are the top touring-professional golfers of our age. The best golfers in the world call on these sages in this book, sometimes on a daily basis, for advice and counsel. They search constantly for ways to improve. That the touring professionals have the time and desire to spend hours on practice tees and greens is beside the point, which is that they seek and receive instructional help.

Yet most amateurs resist going to see a golf professional, preferring instead to spend several hundred dollars buying a new high-tech, whiz-bang driver in the hope it will help them find the fairway more regularly.

That said, I should admit that while preparing this book, I didn't take a single lesson from any of the golf gurus! Nor did I ask for one—I learned my lesson several years ago. Back then, while preparing to write an article about golf schools, I attended three week-long golf school programs in a month and a half. After working with Jack Lumpkin at the Golf Digest School at Sea Island, Georgia, with short game wizard Phil Rogers at the Grand Cypress Golf Academy in Orlando, and finally at a John Jacobs Academy in Marco Island, Florida, my head was spinning. Although each of the schools had me hitting balls with authority, grappling to remember who said what utterly confused me, forcing a visit to Chuck Hogan, who pulled me out of the fog.

So even though I have not personally benefited from the accumulated wisdom of the golf gurus (at least in terms of golf instruction), I wish to acknowledge their gracious willingness to take time from their busy schedules to tell me their stories. All of the gurus were friendly, cooperative, and forthcoming, and whatever success I have had in compiling their stories is due in large part to their willingness to share their experiences.

I would also like to acknowledge the cooperation and assistance of my employers and fellow staffers at *Golfweek*, who were generous and supportive as I wrestled this project to completion. *Golfweek* truly is "America's Golf Newspaper."

Chapter One

A History of Teaching Golf

The game of golf likely began when a Scottish shepherd, bored with watching his charges on the windy, hummocky dunes lands, turned his shepherd's crook upside down and took a swing at a round pebble on the beach.

It's unrecorded but equally likely that the history of golf instruction began when the shepherd's friend immediately came running over to him crying, "Nae Angus...keep th' left ayrm straight, laddie!"

In the centuries since, literally millions of would-be golfers around the world have struggled to master the skills that will propel a small hard ball through the air in search of a target buried in the earth. And that constant struggle has provided steady employment to thousands of men and women who possess the talent to look at a

golf swing and make some constructive recommenda-
tions for improvement.

Still, the concept of a teaching professional as a
specialist, one who does nothing but teach and instruct
golfers, is a relatively new development in the game. For
centuries golf professionals wore many and varied hats;
the actual teaching of the game was perhaps the least
important of their duties. In the old days, as the game
spread across the globe from the ancient linksland of
Scotland, golf professionals were called on to be keepers
of the green, makers of clubs and balls, arrangers of
games, combatants for greater glory in fierce interclub
rivalries and, lastly, teachers.

Around the middle of the nineteenth century, golf
instruction became largely an imitative discipline. Golfers
learning the game or seeking improvement simply copied
the effective swings of the great professional models of the
day: Allan Robertson, longtime pro at St. Andrews; Old
Tom Morris and his ill-fated son, Young Tom, who lived
first at Prestwick and then St. Andrews; and their great
Edinburgh rivals, the Parks and the Dunns.

All of the early swings were largely products of the
equipment of the day and the need to make that equipment work. Golfers played with featherie balls, orbs of
horsehide stuffed full of goose feathers and down. Their
clubs featured extralong wooden shafts with heavy club-
heads of steel and iron.

The earliest swings, therefore, featured an extremely closed stance, with the left foot well advanced and the right withdrawn, to enable the golfer to move the long shaft back and around. The left arm was usually bent almost to right angles on the backswing, wrapping the club around the head far past parallel. The through swing was usually a flat and wristy poke designed to promote the low, hard draw on the ball that would allow it to battle the usually gusty Scottish winds and roll on the hard undulating fairways. As the game moved south into England, golfers started adopting the style common in cricket, where a batsman used a defensive, wristy, batting swing to knock the ball away.

The first book of golf instruction ever published was H.B. Farnie's *The Golfer's Manual*, which was printed in 1857 in Britain. Farnie divided golfers into two classes, the agile and the nonagile, but his book included mainly a discussion of the uses of various golf clubs, along with commentary on the playing styles of the well-known golfing stars of the mid-nineteenth century. Dr. J.G. Macpherson of St. Andrews later wrote *Golf and Golfers*, but again, the volume was short on actual teaching and featured mainly the exploits of Old Tom Morris and the other heroes of St. Andrews.

Meaningful changes didn't occur until the old featherie balls were supplanted by the gutta percha balls. Guttas, made from the rubberized sap of a tree, came into vogue in the late nineteenth century; the golf swing slowly began to adapt to this new technology. Featheries came off the clubface with a liveliness not unlike today's modern balls, but they did not carry as well in the air, especially in the wind. So, swings were designed to produce the low, running draws that made featheries most effective. Gutta balls, on the other hand, flew through the air much better, so the key became getting the ball airborne.

Golfers began to realize that producing such a ball flight would require a different swing plane, one more upright and open, to deliver the descending blow needed to get a gutta into the air and flying.

In 1891, Horace Hutchinson authored what was probably the last golfing manifesto promoting anything resembling a closed stance. He held that the correct stance for golf was now more of a square alignment, with the left foot advanced only a few inches ahead of the right. But the great English champion John Ball, who played at the Royal Liverpool club at Hoylake, rendered Hutchinson's ideas obsolete by winning British Amateurs and Opens by the bushel using an open stance, playing the ball further back in his stance, and creating high, soft, pitch shots.

Following Ball's lead was Harry Vardon, who was also an open-stance player. Vardon, of course, left his imprint on the game with its next technological advance: the overlapping finger grip, which today bears his name and is almost universally used. The innovation of the Vardon grip was to bring the two hands together on the club and mold them into one unit. By holding a club at that one point, rather than split apart, the player was able to gain maximum centrifugal leverage during the swing, especially at the moment of the strike.

With the advent of the Vardon grip, the golfing world was ready for the coming of the rubber-core ball, a turn-of-the-century development. This new ball combined the jump-off-the-face property of the featherie with the bore-through-the-air qualities of the gutta. And when steel shafts joined the technological mix in the 1930s, golfers found they could change their swings to a shorter, more controlled path to the ball.

But technological advancements that shaped golf swings were just part of the development of golf instruction. Much innovation in the field occurred when the game moved across the Atlantic to America, around 1888. Once established, Americans took to golf with their usual enthusiasm, and as the game grew in popularity, the need for qualified teachers grew with it.

The first two instructional books published in the New World, James Lee's *Golf in America: A Practical Manual* in 1895; and H.J. Whigham's *How To Play Golf* in 1897, both taught the long and flat St. Andrean swing. But Whigham encouraged teachers to study their students' individual swings and discern between "errors of skill" and "errors of emotion."

Golf's popularity mushroomed following a turn-of-the-century barnstorming tour of America by two members of Britain's Great Triumvirate: Harry Vardon and J.H. Taylor. The third member, James Braid, had a deathly fear of ocean travel (not to mention a dislike of automobiles and telephones) and stayed home. These three men were in the midst of a twenty-year dominance of professional golf; in a twenty-one-year period, only three other men won the British Open.

The tour of America was a raging success, drawing swollen crowds to watch the two great men give swing clinics and demonstrations, play exhibition matches against local heroes, and compete in America's championships (Vardon won the U.S. Open in 1900; Taylor finished second). At one heavily attended stop in Boston, Vardon was hitting shots indoors into a net. Bored with the exercise, he began to take aim at a water valve handle sticking out through the netting. A nervous store manager finally begged Vardon to stop after he had hit the valve so many times the manager feared a deluge.

A popular product sold at these appearances was the stereopticon viewer, which showed the masters' swings in sequential motion. Newspapers and magazines wrote article after article about the two men, describing their swings in detail and explaining to hungry readers why they dominated the game. But the public wanted more. Vardon responded with *The Complete Golfer* in 1905, which was probably the first "how I do it" instructional book penned by a golfing great.

The Vardon-Taylor barnstorming tours also led to heightened demand for teachers. From the home of golf, Scotland, emerged the first wave of what became a steady flow of golf instructors. As new golf clubs were built, first in the Northeast and then everywhere from Georgia to Chicago, the call went back to the homeland for golf professionals. Many answered; Willie Anderson, Willie Park Jr., and Willie Dunn Jr. were among them. They were assigned to the pro shops, fixed and made clubs, maintained the grounds, hired and trained caddies, and managed to find time to teach the game to the sons and daughters of the members. A young Donald Ross began his American career as a golf pro in Massachusetts after emigrating from Dornoch. He eventually settled in Pinehurst, North Carolina, where he started building golf courses and became the preeminent golf course architect of his era.

One Scottish town that produced a staggering number of golf professionals in America was Carnoustie, just across the Firth of Tay from St. Andrews. Indeed, one family, all sons of the greenskeeper at Carnoustie, sent five men to America to find fame and fortune as players and teachers of the ancient game. Alex, Willie, Macdonald, George, and Jimmy Smith all served as professionals at clubs around the United States.

The most prominent of the Smiths and one of the most influential early teaching specialists was Alexander. Born in 1874, Smith first served as golf professional in England at the Luton, and later St. Neots, golf clubs in the mid-1890s. He returned to Carnoustie to work for a year in the clubmaking shop of Bob Simpson before heading a cross the ocean to America in 1898 with four other pros from St. Andrews. His first job was on the staff of the Washington Park Golf Club in Chicago, where he taught, patched together broken hickory shafts, and made a name for himself by winning golf tournaments: the Western Open twice, three California Opens, and four Metropolitan Opens, among others.

But it was his performance in a series of U.S. Opens that brought him national acclaim. He finished second in 1898 and 1901, fourth in 1903, second in 1905, and, finally, first in 1906 at Onwentsia in Lake Forest, Illinois. (His brother Willie had won the Open in 1899, making the Smiths the first, and so far only, brothers to win the U.S. Open.)

Smith's impressive showings enabled him to move from Chicago to the country's richest and most prestigious club jobs: Nassau Country Club in Glen Cove, New York; Wykagyl Club in New Rochelle; and finally Shennecossett in New London, Connecticut. By 1925, with this experience—and his U.S. Open triumphs—Smith could pretty much write his own ticket, and he did. He split summers working at Shennecossett and the new Westchester Biltmore Country Club in Rye, New York; he taught during winters at the Belleaire Country Club near Tampa and the Miami Biltmore resort.

After his Open win in 1906, Smith followed Vardon's lead and wrote *Lessons in Golf*, firmly setting the pattern of golf champions penning instructional manuals.

"Golf is a science," he wrote, "and not a bag of tricks." The book was wildly successful and solidified Smith's position as the foremost teacher of the game in the United States.

That reputation was enhanced by the number of champions Smith produced. One of his early students at Nassau was Jerome Travers, who won the U.S. Open (1915) and four U.S. Amateur crowns. At Shennecossett one of Smith's regulars was Glenna Collett Vare, who would follow her teacher south to Florida in the winters. Gene Sarazen called Vare "the greatest 'taught' golfer we've ever seen in this country." Smith shortened Vare's backswing and made her putting stroke more compact. With these improvements, she went on to win an unmatched six U.S. Women's Amateur titles.

Smith also tutored the inimitable Walter Hagen, a winner of eleven major titles in his storied career. Indeed, the two were of a kind, as Smith was noted for his raffish sense of humor and gregarious nature. In addition to the groundbreaking work he did as a golfing professional and the legacy of his work handed down by his famous pupils, Alexander Smith is most remembered for his oft-quoted advice on putting: "Miss 'em quick!"

In 1919 Jim Barnes, winner of the first two PGA Championships, lent his name to the book *Picture Analysis of Golf Strokes*, a groundbreaking volume that used modern advances in photography to capture the golf swing in sequential form. Featuring full-page layouts of Barnes' swing, the book made a significant contribution to golf instruction by allowing students to examine the parts of the swing, making it more easy to imitate.

In 1922, Seymour Dunn, a Scottish-born golf professional, published *Golf Fundamentals*, which took Barnes' idea one step farther. Dunn superimposed lines designating the proper swing plane and allowing the viewer to see both correct and incorrect swings.

The great Bobby Jones once wrote, "The best luck I ever had in golf was when Stewart Maiden came from Carnoustie, Scotland, to be professional at the East Lake Club." Jones, who grew up in Atlanta, Georgia, noted the succession of Carnoustie professionals who worked at the famous East Lake Club where he learned the game: Alex Smith, Jimmy Maiden, Stewart Maiden, Willie Ogg, and Charlie Gray.

In his literate autobiography, *Down the Fairway*, Jones noted how he picked up the game by accompanying his parents to the course, where he would closely watch the distinctive swing of the Carnoustie man, Stewart Maiden. "When I followed Stewart, I didn't even carry one club," Jones wrote. "I just watched him. I never was conscious of studying his play or of trying to play like him."

Jones claimed he never took a formal lesson from Maiden but just enjoyed watching him play the game. Yet it is obvious that he adopted the style of his mentor one way or another. He writes of an incident at the Roebuck Country Club in Birmingham, Alabama, where he was a fifteen-year-old prodigy.

"I was playing a practice round before that tournament, and this man, who had not seen Stewart since he
left Carnoustie, was standing by Dad as I was driving off
the tenth tee in the distance.

'When did Stewart Maiden get here?' he inquired.

'Dad told him Stewart was not there at all.

'You can't fool me,' was the rejoinder. 'I saw
Stewart drive just now from the tenth tee. Think I don't
know that old Carnoustie swing?'

'Nevertheless,' Dad told him, 'that happens to be
my son Rob under that swing.'"

Jones and his Carnoustie swing, of course, went on
to completely dominate the golf world during the 1920s.
He won the U.S. Open four times (finishing second three
other times) and the U.S. Amateur five times in seven
years. In 1930 he captured the Impregnable Quadrilateral:
the British Open and Amateur and the U.S. Open and
Amateur. He then quit competitive golf.

When he retired, despite his international fame,
Bobby Jones needed money; he had played as an amateur
his entire career. He took a job representing the Spalding
Company, wrote two books, *Bobby Jones on Golf* and *Golf
is My Game*, and ventured to Hollywood to produce a
series of short films on golf instruction. The films were
advanced for the day, with slow-motion footage showing
Jones's rhythmic swing and the use of other special effects
to demonstrate portions of his swing motion. They were
supremely popular, shown as preludes to the featured picture of the week. Jones's series, however, eventually land-

ed in a dusty vault until a few years ago when they were rediscovered and turned into a bestselling video package.

Due in no small part to the incredible celebrity of figures like Bobby Jones and Walter Hagen, golf entered its golden age in the Roaring Twenties. And golf instructors, in contrast to generalist golf professionals, began sprouting up around the country.

One of the most unorthodox figures had to be Ernest Jones, the one-legged "professional from Fifth Avenue." Born in Manchester, England, he apprenticed to a clubmaker at age twelve, following his father's death. Jones moved up through the ranks, played well in several British Opens, and was eventually named professional at the Chislehurst Golf Club.

While serving in England's Sportsman's Battalion in France during World War I, he lost his leg to a grenade. Legend has it that on the first day out of the hospital, Jones tried to play a round of golf.

His injury forced him to rethink the golf swing. He learned that if he ignored the shaft and concentrated on moving the clubhead instead, he could keep his balance and make solid contact with the ball. He likened the swing to the way one would control a weight tied to the end of a string. In 1921, fitted with an artificial leg, Ernest Jones set the course record of 64 at Chislehurst.

In short order, he was off to America, where he was invited to serve as instructor at the newly formed Women's National Golf & Tennis Club on Long Island. There, he worked more on his unusual swing theory.

Jones said the swing was essentially a circle and that a true swing would return to the point from which it started, namely, the ball. Thus, he deduced the imperative in golf was not to try to hit the ball, but merely to "swing the clubhead." Jones called his swing an accelerated pendulum. He never bothered with backswings, weight shifts, wrist cocks or any other individual parts. "You can't divide the swing into parts and still have a swing," he would say. "A cat is a cat. If you dissect it, you'll have blood and guts and bones all over. But you won't have a cat."

Jones eventually took his theories to a studio in a fifth-floor brownstone walk-up in Manhattan, where he was booked solid for months in advance at the price of $5 per half-hour. His methods were viciously attacked by other teaching professionals. He was invited once to speak at a PGA convention in Minnesota: the other pros debated with him for two hours. "Your system is too simple," Horton Smith told him "We wouldn't sell enough lessons."

"That's the trouble," Jones said. "You want your pupils to go on suffering. Once you get people to swing the clubhead, it will grow on them."

Jones preferred to end his day in a saloon with a whiskey and lemon juice and with lengthy dissertations about his swing-the-clubhead theory, which he'd demonstrate with a cane. When pressed (or after a second dram), he could be talked into reciting a poem that underlined his simple theories:

> A centipede was happy quite,
> Until a toad in fun

Said "Pray, which leg goes after which?"
That worked her mind to such a pitch
She lay distracted in a ditch,
Considering how to run.

In the early 1930s steel shafts began to replace the traditional hickory ones, setting up a major change not only in equipment, but in the way the game was played and taught. Steel shafts did not torque, or twist, during the swing as much as hickory did, so that players had more control during the swing. Because steel was not as whippy as the hickory shaft, perfect timing was no longer of paramount importance. This allowed golfers to swing harder and still maintain a high degree of control.

As a result, golf swings became more upright, along the target line. Players were taught to reduce the influence of the hands at the apex of the swing and utilize an arms-and-shoulders swing instead.

One of the first elite players to adjust to the new equipment and this modern swing was Byron Nelson. Growing up in Fort Worth, Texas, alongside Ben Hogan (the two started out as caddies at Glen Gate Country Club), Nelson was a pioneer with steel, and he changed a handsy swing to one that made more use of the arms and legs.

In 1932 teaching pro Alex Morrison published *A New Way To Better Golf*, which was one of the first instructionals to encompass the new shaft technology. Morrison preached that the new clubs required a swing powered by the muscles of the left side, with the left shoulder and arm driving the swing. Morrison's left-side swing tended to deliver a more descending blow into the ball, rather than the more sweeping swing of a right-side player. On America's soft, inland courses, where the high-flying, soft-landing ball of a Morrison-inspired swing was beneficial, his theories were adopted far and wide.

Morrison's driving, left-side swing was utilized by most of the great players of the Depression era: Hogan, Nelson and Snead were all left-side golfers. But in 1953 Tommy Armour, known as the Silver Scot, published a contrary view.

Armour was a native Scotsman who emigrated in the early 1920s, turned professional, and won the U.S. Open in 1927 at Oakmont Country Club in Pennsylvania. He went on to win the PGA Championship in 1930, the British Open in 1931, and many other championships before concentrating on teaching. He worked at a variety of northeastern clubs and spent most winters working out of the Boca Raton Club in Florida. There, he had a long waiting list of both touring professionals and ordinary hackers. He would sit under a colorful umbrella, sip his favorite beverage and turn his keen eye on the swings of those laboring before him.

He held that a golfer should "whack the hell out of the ball with the right hand." The left side, he believed, was for guidance only. Since the right hand was closer to the ball, he thought it should control the action. Plus, most golfers were right-handed, so the traditional left-side theory would feel unnatural to them. His book, *How To Play Your Best Golf All The Time,* was a great success when it was published in 1953.

In 1957 Ben Hogan attempted to bridge the gap between the two theories with the publication of *Five Lessons: The Modern Fundamentals of Golf,* written with Herbert Warren Wind and illustrated by Anthony Ravielli. Hogan posited that neither left- nor right-side dominance was all that important. Hogan instructed his readers to adjust their traditional Vardon grips so that there was more pressure on the last three fingers of the left hand and the middle two of the right. He also recommended pointing the toes of the right foot perpendicular to the target line at address to help restrict the hip turn and increase the length of the backswing.

He explained one move that had helped him overcome chronic pull-hooking into a swing, which produced a power fade. The technique involved a roll of the hands that opened the clubface to the maximum on the backswing. He called it "pronating." From that position he couldn't get the clubface closed at impact, no matter how hard he tried, thus preventing the turned-over hook that had so plagued him early in his career.

But the most important contribution of Hogan's seminal book, which sells robustly even today, was his illustration of the swing plane as a "pane of glass." Hogan tried to swing back parallel to an imaginary glass pane tilted from his shoulders down to the ball and to keep his club just under this pane on the downswing as his hips turned into the ball. With this image in mind, golfers could find their own personal swing plane based on their own height and tendencies instead of trying to imitate other golfers' swings.

Hogan's book coincided with golf's next popularity boom, a boom driven by television. By the late 1950s, television was an integral part of golf's landscape. Most major events were televised, meaning new found popularity for the game's best, such as Arnold Palmer and Jack Nicklaus. Plus golfers could now study the swings of their heroes on the tube, instead of attending tournaments and tromping through the rough. An early program, "Shell's Wonderful World of Golf," featured swing analyses in slow motion with commentary by Gene Sarazen, as well as swing tips from the players.

Also in the 1950s and early '60s, popular golf magazines began to focus more and more on golf instruction. The magazines' research had long shown that the main reason subscribers picked up the glossy monthlies was to soak in the swing tips of the month. Demographics indicated that the typical subscriber was a high-handicapper, and editors of the monthlies were instructed to give their readers tips, tips, and more tips.

That editorial philosophy created the need for instructors and qualified writers. Although the magazines always tried to sign up the most popular touring pros for lucrative instructional articles, they also relied on a cadre of experienced teaching professionals who came from the traditional ranks of club jobs.

In 1971, *Golf Digest* magazine, the leading golf publication, asked Bob Toski and Dick Aultman to set up a program of instructional schools that they could offer to their readers. Instruction by the playing editors would be featured in the magazine. Toski and Aultman, who recruited other teaching pros, notably Jim Flick, worked on developing a standardized and simple method of communicating the difficulties of the golf swing to their audience of high-handicap golfers. The subsequent Golf Digest Golf Schools helped launch an entire industry of resort-based golf schools, typically featuring a week of instruction for a large group of golfers and a faculty of teachers imported to work on various aspects of the game. Toski and Flick later published a book, *How to Become a Complete Golfer*, that distilled the simplified, basic code of golf instruction they had developed while teaching *Golf Digest* subscribers.

From the sequential still photos of Jim Barnes's 1919 book to Bobby Jones's imaginative use of film in the early 1930s, photography had long played an important role in golf instruction. Teachers moved from slow-motion filming to the new technology of videotape in the early 1970s, finding that the instant playback capabilities of video were greatly beneficial to practice tee usage. Video quickly became the standard technique for swing analysis and remains so today. New digital technology permits a teaching professional to use a video camera to capture images that can be stored in a computer and printed out instantly on paper for analysis and comparison.

Although great golfers have always relied on a swing mentor for reinforcement or fine-tuning, it is only in the last two decades that touring professionals have come to see the resource of a personal teaching pro to be of paramount importance. The "swing guru" who becomes part of a PGA Tour pro's entourage is a recent development.

The real work of teaching golf continues to take place day in and day out at private clubs, public driving ranges, and practice tees everywhere: at golf schools, seminars, and in individual lessons from the thousands of members of the PGA of America. The PGA of America now sponsors an annual "teaching summit," at which the growing legion of teaching specialists can assemble to discuss swing theories and teaching techniques and honor the PGA Teacher of the Year. This award was inaugurated in 1986 to honor the outstanding teachers from the ranks of the PGA of America and is based on a teacher's record as an innovator, articles or books he or she has written, and the success rate of his or her pupils.

The thirst for knowledge about the golf swing remains both deep and unquenched. Golf instructional books and videos perennially rank among the bestselling sports volumes; golf resorts across the country have built elaborate practice ranges and vie to recruit big name teaching professionals to set up golf academies; and parents search for golf camps and junior academies with the same zeal they once used to get their children into Ivy League schools.

The history of teaching golf has shown that changes in technology have always led to changes in golf swings and the way the game is played and taught. Because technology plays such a pivotal role in the game today, one can only imagine what the typical swing and the common lesson will be in the twenty-first century.

Chapter Two

THE HARMONS

A TEACHING DYNASTY

Sons following fathers into the same business is always a dicey proposition. Although there are occasional success stories of dynasties that last into the next generation, there are probably more failures. If the father is successful, the son seems either not to measure up or to try too hard to do so.

It's all the more remarkable, then, that Claude Harmon, one of the most successful, well-known and highly regarded teaching professionals of the last generation, has been succeeded by not one, not two, but four of his sons. All are teachers, all are club professionals, and in their own ways, all are as successful as their father.

In fact, Claude Harmon could be said to have more than just his four sons (and two daughters) following his lead. In his late years, Harmon worked with budding young professionals Steve Elkington and Blaine McCallister. He often joked that they were the only of his sons who could play. And in his long years as head golf professional at Winged Foot in Mamaroneck, New York, Harmon trained a list of assistant professionals which reads as a virtual who's who of golf in the last thirty years: Dave Marr, Jackie Burke Jr., Mike Souchak, Dick Mayer, Ron Funseth, and many others.

His four sons, of course, grew up living a life of golf. It was a nomadic existence: they spent half the year in New York and the other half in either Florida or Palm Springs. Yet it was also exciting. The guest at the dinner table might be Ben Hogan one night, Tommy Armour the next. Dave Marr baby-sat for the boys. Out on the practice range, one might find Claude working with a PGA player or a President of the United States.

"We were always around great golf courses and great people," says oldest son, Butch Harmon. "That was one of the things that encouraged the four of us to stay in the game and pursue a career in it."

Claude Harmon was born in Savannah, but grew up near the Dubsdread golf course in Orlando, Florida. He turned professional in his teen years, and began his life-long pursuit of the warm sun: winters in the south and summers in the north. His first club job was at the North Shore Golf Club in Chicago, where he worked for Jack Grout and Ky Laffoon. He then moved to Lochmoor in Detroit as head professional, and later served as assistant head pro under Craig Wood at Winged Foot before moving up to the head professional's job there.

Like many club professionals of his era, Harmon tried his hand at playing the professional tour in his prime. But like many of his fellow pros, he found that the economic demands of raising a family precluded the life of constant travel and play for uncertain results.

Still, Harmon was a player. He not only set course records of 61 at Winged Foot and 60 at the Seminole Golf Club in North Palm Beach, Fla., but won the 1948 Masters at Augusta by five strokes, setting a tournament record. He usually played well at the then-match-play PGA Championship, making the semifinals three times and the quarterfinals twice more. When the U.S. Open came to Winged Foot in 1959, the forty-two-year-old Harmon, host pro, finished in a tie for third.

But Harmon gave up most of his touring life in 1945, when he became head golf professional at the prestigious Winged Foot, a job he held until 1977. For twelve years, he took his family to Florida in the winter, where he held the head pro job at Seminole. In 1959, no doubt influenced by one of his favorite students, President Dwight Eisenhower, Harmon moved his winter home to the Thunderbird Country Club near Palm Springs. That he worked at three of the most prestigious and elite country clubs in the land is an indication of the esteem in which Claude Harmon was held as a teaching professional. Although he often worked with kings, presidents, and celebrities of every stripe, he was just as happy working on the range with a high-handicap member.

Harmon considered the one-swing-fits-all philosophy ridiculous. He would size up a golfer's ability and body and reshape the swing to fit. "If there is a strong suit that my brothers and I have as teachers, it is something we picked up from Dad, and that's to teach everyone as an individual," Butch Harmon says. "If you look at the physical make-up of golfers, they are all different. They have different sizes, shapes, weights, degrees of flexibility, strength. Other than the basic fundamentals, you have to treat each player as an individual, look at what they can and can't do and try to improve on the things they can't do."

Harmon was also one of the first teaching pros to embrace the technology of videotape. He believed that golfers think in pictures more than in words, and found video helpful in showing a golfer the basic why's and how's of what he was trying to explain. He would study film of the greats (Hogan, Byron Nelson, Snead, Jimmy Demaret, Tommy Armour and Craig Wood) and often freeze-frame it and trace certain positions on the dining-room wall.

But he never strayed far from the fundamentals, and always managed to hone in on the basic problems in a golfer's swings. "If a person has a rash and a wart and a ruptured appendix, you don't worry about the wart and the rash," he would say.

His eye was legendary. "Greatest eye I've ever seen," says son Butch. "He'd know what to do after you hit one shot." He always said he was not trying to teach golf to people, but to teach people to play golf. He taught his sons to watch the ball and to learn why it reacted to a swing the way it did. Son Craig remembered, "What we got from our Dad was the ability to find that one thing in the swing that caused eight other things to go wrong. He taught us to keep asking the question: why is this happening?"

His methods were usually successful. Few Harmon pupils left the practice tee without a smile on their lips. For Claude Harmon, in addition to being one of the greatest golf instructors of his age, was also one of the greatest raconteurs. He was a storyteller, a needler, the ultimate hail-fellow-well-met. At the Seminole Golf Club, when Harmon began to hold court, the word went out, and his audience on a typical day might include Henry Ford II, the Duke of Windsor and businessman Marshall Field. At Augusta, even after Harmon stopped playing, he still held court in the players' lounge for hours at a time.

Harmon was involved in a famous and oft-repeated golf story concerning his good friend Ben Hogan. The two were paired in the Masters one year. When they came to the fearful par-three 12th hole, Harmon stepped up and made an ace, to the delighted roar of the crowd. Hogan, in his usual deep reverie of concentration, said nothing, until after he had rolled in a putt for a birdie two. "You know Claude," Hogan then reportedly said, "That's the first time I've ever birdied that hole!"

Harmon, who worked with presidents and celebrities, befriended King Hassan II of Morocco, a noted golf enthusiast. Upon the king's invitation, Harmon visited the North African nation dozens of times to give private lessons to the king. There are reports from Harmon's contemporaries that he received lavish gifts for his services, such as automobiles and boxes of jewels. He also mined his experiences in North Africa for a few good stories. When in Morocco, Harmon played every day with the king. Almost invariably, the king would ask Harmon for a club selection recommendation. Harmon would give his opinion, the king would select one club less, and almost always his approach would fall one shot one club short of the green. Finally one day, when the king had ignored Harmon's suggestion to hit an eight-iron and dumped his nine-iron shot into a bunker, Harmon approached the king.

"Your Majesty, I've been teaching you for ten years, but there is one thing I've neglected to teach you," he said. "It is this: the ball and the club do not know that you are the king. Even you, Your Majesty, have to hit enough club."

Luckily, the king laughed.

There was not much laughing going on in July 1971, however, when Harmon and several other pros were in attendance at the king's annual golf tournament when a military coup attempt broke out. Marching across the fairways of a seaside course, the rebels began spraying machine-gun fire everywhere as 500 guests dived for safety. When a man standing next to Harmon was gunned down, he hit the deck, and tried to crawl to safety, only to be kicked and butted by the rebel troops. He said later that it was only because he was wearing a yellow golf shirt, reportedly the color that signified sympathy with the rebels, that he was not shot. Several hundred others were killed before the king's troops put down the rebellion.

Certainly, Claude Harmon's most enduring legacy is his four sons, all of whom followed him into the golf business to become teaching professionals. His oldest son, Butch, (Claude Harmon Jr.) is now head golf professional at Lochinvar Golf Club in Houston and works with the likes of both Greg Norman and Tiger Woods. Craig Harmon (named after Claude's longtime friend and mentor Craig Wood) has been head golf professional at Rochester's prestigious Oak Hill Country Club for more than twenty years. He works with touring pros such as Jeff Sluman and Cathy Morse. Dick Harmon has been head pro at Houston's River Oaks Country Club since the 1970s, and has worked with Lanny Wadkins, Fred Couples, and Craig Stadler. The youngest Harmon, Billy, became head pro at the prestigious Newport Country Club in 1990, and works with Jay Haas, Curtis Strange, Billy Andrade, and others.

If there is a dark side to the Claude Harmon story, it is that he was a stern taskmaster with his four golfing sons. Although some said that if Harmon weren't needling you it meant he didn't like you, he was inordinately rough on his kids, at least in public.

Once, for instance, he said that his eldest son, Butch, who struggled on the PGA Tour for a few years, was "the only pro in America who shoots letters instead of numbers: WD, DNF, NC, OB, PU. He carries a can of alphabet soup in his golf bag."

Another time, he watched son Billy, who five times failed to get his PGA Tour card, hit balls for thirty minutes on the practice tee. When Billy asked what his Dad thought, he was told, "Ringling Brothers brings over elephants from Africa, and if they can't do the fox trot or learn tricks in four or five weeks, they send them back. But there's no place I can send you; I've been telling you the same thing for twenty-five years and you haven't listened to me yet."

Yet another time, he observed son Dick giving a lesson to Lanny Wadkins. "You're going to tell this guy how to play and you can't even break 80?" he demanded. "Dick, the only thing you can tell this guy is to change his route to the bank every day. The only thing you can do is screw him up."

The boys responded to Harmon's tough love in different ways. Butch, the oldest, left home at nineteen and went his own way. Billy, the youngest, was rebellious: he would work as an assistant in Claude's pro shop, get fired, leave to work at clubs far away from home, and eventually come back to relive the cycle. On the other hand, both Craig and Dick had reasonably comfortable relationships with their father.

"Our father was somewhat difficult," Butch Harmon says today. "His philosophy was to beat you down and irritate you so much that you'd work all the harder to prove to him you could do things. Right or wrong, it was the way his father had raised him."

Butch had perhaps the toughest time, being his father's namesake. "It was very difficult being the oldest and having the same name as such a famous father," he says. "If you played good, people would say, 'Well, he should be a good player: after all, Claude Harmon is his father.' And If you played poorly, they'd all say 'Can you believe how bad he is?. . . his father is Claude Harmon!' A lot of times it was a no-win situation."

But even Butch admits that being Claude Harmon Jr. also opened a lot of doors in his career. In the end, both he and brother Billy, despite the rocky parts of their parental relationship, came to understand their father, and both ended up being close to him.

After his unique childhood in golf, Butch turned pro in 1965 while he was in the U.S. Army, stationed in Alaska. He thought he would make a little pocket money giving golf lessons to his fellow soldiers. Butch went on to serve a tour of duty in Vietnam, and when he returned, he worked for two years as one of Claude's assistants at Winged Foot.

He qualified for the PGA Tour in 1968 and played through 1971 without much success. He did win the inaugural B.C. Open in 1971, appeared in a few Opens, and although he was never a top-level star, did earn enough money to keep his Tour card. "In 1971," he says, "I did the Tour a favor and left!" His oldest daughter was coming of school age that year, and Butch decided that if he wasn't going to make a living on Tour, then it was time for him to get serious and find a secure club pro job.

Ironically, perhaps, his first pro job was in Morocco, following in his father's footsteps as private golf pro to King Hassan II. He lived with his family in Rabat until 1975, then came back to the United States and took a job at Crow Valley Country Club in Bettendorf, Iowa. In 1980, he moved to Texas and has been there since.

He worked for some time with Jay Rivera and his old baby-sitter Dave Marr in a golf course design and construction firm, and later ran a municipal course in Texas City for several years. He then started the Harmon School of Golf at the Cypresswood Golf Club, and in 1992 he finally landed the job as head golf professional at the Lochinvar Golf Club near Houston, an exclusive, golf-only club.

He began working with tour professionals in 1988. Steve Elkington was his first client, but he was always more friend than client. The young Australian attended college at the University of Houston, where Butch first met him. They became friends and Elkington was virtually adopted by the Harmon family. Claude, who was in semi-retirement as professional emeritus at Lochinvar, took the young Elkington under his wing, and both he and Butch worked with him. Elkington joined the Tour in 1987 and quickly established himself as one of its bright young stars.

In 1990, Davis Love III began working with Butch, and the following year, on Elkington's recommendation,

Greg Norman came calling. In 1991, Norman was suffering a slump. Despite numerous worldwide victories, he was discouraged and at a personal low point. Larry Mize had chipped in on him to win the '87 Masters, Bob Tway had sunk that bunker shot on him at the PGA Championship in '86, and in '89, Mark Calcavecchia had beaten him in a playoff for the British Open at Royal Troon. Norman was beginning to feel like golf's bridesmaid.

Butch Harmon was ready for him. He had long been an admirer of Norman's game, studying his swing in some depth even before he met the Australian star.

"I had formed my own opinion of what I'd do if I ever had a chance to work with Greg Norman," Butch says. "When I got that chance, I had a game plan all ready. So it was easy to sit down with him, show him some film of his old swing and the way he was swinging now and show him the things I thought he needed to change and what his flaws were. We both agreed that what I saw and what was happening were things he didn't like, and we took it from there."

Like many teachers who work with one golfer over a period of years, Harmon never changes the message of his lessons dramatically. He and Norman work on the same things over and over. "It doesn't matter who you are or how good or bad a player you are, your flaws will always be the same. Your tendencies will be the same," he says. "So I watch film of Greg whether I'm at a tournament with him or just taping from television, and I constantly go back over it. I talk to his caddie, Tony Navarro, about what happened during a certain round if I'm not there. It's just making sure he doesn't fall back into some of his old habits. "

Harmon thinks Greg Norman is the hardest worker he's ever seen on Tour, and considers it one of the major parts of his job to see that Norman works on the right things. "He has really elevated his game to another level in the last few years," he says. "I don't think anyone in the world is even close." He remembered a conversation with a golf reporter after the 1995 NEC World Series of Golf, which Norman won after chipping in from seventy feet on the last hole. "He said it was nice that Greg was finally getting a break after all that's happened to him in his career, and I said the rest of the world better watch out if Greg Norman starts getting breaks!"

But the teacher is ever alert to Norman's traditional bad habits. His worst mistake, says Harmon, is sliding too far forward with his hips in the downswing. He gets the club moving too far inside going back, and when he slides his hips, the club gets stuck behind, resulting in a pushed shot.

To combat this, Harmon tells Norman to work hard on making sure the club doesn't get too far inside on the backswing, as well as the rotation of the lower body and footwork to keep those sliding hips in control. "The plane of his swing has changed so much, too," Harmon says. "It used to be an upright and steep kind of swing, but now it's much flatter which shallows him out at the ball and makes it easier for him to control his distance with his short irons."

Harmon admires Greg Norman's mental toughness. "He does nothing in moderation," he says. "He's a full-bore type of guy; it's the way he approaches golf, workout routines, the time he's on his boat or fishing—everything he does is at 110 percent. I think that's why he's so good. He's very aggressive when he plays golf, sure, and he's lost tournaments because he's aggressive. But that's the only way he knows how to play, and if he tried to play any other way, I don't think he'd be as good as he is."

Harmon also works with Davis Love III, who, he notes, has an entirely different personality on and off the golf course. Love is more laid-back, but he still can muster a competitive drive when forced. And after a poor 1994 season Love needed a kick in the pants. "1994 was probably the best thing that ever happened to Davis," says Harmon. "He had gotten a little lazy and a little complacent. He had won a lot of money at an early age, and he pretty much quit working on his golf game. So '94 was a wake-up call, and he has worked harder on his game than he has in years. And it shows. If it wasn't for what was probably an act of God and Ben Crenshaw, he would have won the '95 Masters, and if he putts at all, he wins the '95 U.S. Open at Shinnecock."

One Harmon student whose best golf may yet be in front of him is Eldrick (Tiger) Woods, the Stanford collegian and two-time U.S. Amateur champion. Harmon first met Tiger Woods during the 1993 Amateur, at the

Champions Golf Club in Houston. After he lost in an early round, his father brought him to Lochinvar for a lesson; Harmon and Woods have been working closely together ever since.

"What I enjoy with Tiger is seeing how much he's improved in just a short period of time," Harmon says. He recalls that in the spring of 1995, when Woods made his heralded debut at the Masters, he out-drove everyone in the field, but couldn't hit an eight- or nine-iron on the green, much less close to the pins. Barely five months later, however, at the U.S. Amateur at the Newport Country Club in Rhode Island, Woods won his second straight national amateur title by going down the shaft, taking distance off some irons, hitting softer approaches, and otherwise playing with new-found finesse. Woods captured the title with a beautiful eight-iron approach on the 36th hole that ended up three feet from the pin.

"That's what was so incredible to me," Harmon says. "How much better he had gotten from April to August. People tend to forget this kid is just twenty years old. He is going to get better and better each year, which is a scary thought. I think he has a chance to become one of the truly great players of the game—only time will tell if that works out or not."

Butch Harmon sees many parallels between Woods and Norman: they are both dedicated to their games, they are both hard workers, they are both always trying to improve. Woods calls Harmon two or three times a week to describe his practice sessions and ask what needs to be done next. "He has a tremendous desire to get better," Harmon says. "That's what's gonna make him one of the best players in the world."

Younger brother Dick Harmon was born in 1947, the year before his father's Masters win, and he still vividly recalls the nomadic, yet exciting life as the son of a famous club professional. It was not all glamour: he describes the family's winter home at the Seminole Golf Club in Florida as "a small cottage tucked behind the maintenance shed where the greenskeeper worked."

Like his brothers, he tried his hand at competitive golf without much success. One of Dick Harmon's high-water points came in the 1964 U.S. Junior Amateur, when he qualified for match play with a score of 150 for two rounds. Unfortunately, that was the year Johnny Miller set an all-time qualifying score record of 139, and then waltzed untouched through the match-play field to capture the title.

Dick attended San Diego State for a year before turning pro and taking a job at the Waverly Country Club in Portland, Oregon, working with head pro Jack Dawes, who had worked for Claude Harmon at Winged Foot. From there, he followed brother Craig's career path by working at the Lakeside Country Club in North Hollywood, and then as an assistant at Thunderbird with his father until 1977. That year, he accepted the job as head professional at Houston's River Oaks Club, where he still works and teaches today.

Also like his brothers, he began working early on with touring professionals. One of Dick Harmon's first famous students was Lanny Wadkins, who came to Houston in 1985 for some lessons. Something must have worked, for early that year, Wadkins won the Bob Hope Desert Classic at 28 under par, then a few weeks later captured the Los Angeles Open at 20 under, both record scores for those events. "I called Lanny and said 'Why do you need me? You're 54 under par for the month of January!'" Dick remembers. However, later that fall, after Wadkins had been voted PGA Player of the Year, it was Dick Harmon who accepted the trophy for him.

Dick became involved with Fred Couples in the mid 1980s. He had known Couples since the Seattle-born golfer attended the University of Houston in the late 1970s. In 1987, Couples traveled to Houston to play in the Houston Open—or so he thought. When he got to town, he discovered that he had forgotten to commit to play in the event. So instead, he spent the next two weeks at River Oaks, where he and Harmon solidified their working relationship. A week later, he won the Byron Nelson Classic in Dallas.

Couples, of course, is not noted for his dedication to hard work; yet at the same time he is blessed with immense natural talent. Harmon says that from the beginning of their relationship, he's aimed to shorten Couples's long and loose swing and help eliminate his tendency to stand too close to the ball. Even today, when Freddie's game goes on the fritz, one of those two problems is usu-

THE HARMONS: A TEACHING DYNASTY

ally to blame. Couples still asks Dick Harmon to watch him hit balls from time to time, although he works more frequently these days with Paul Marchand, a former assistant to Harmon at River Oaks who now teaches out of the Houston Country Club.

Dick Harmon's third well-known student came on a recommendation from Lanny Wadkins in 1985: Craig Stadler. Another golfer perhaps not well known for his dedication to beating balls, Stadler, too, has enormous talent. Dick's task with Stadler is to lengthen his swing.

"It all goes back to what Dad taught us," he says. "You don't teach one swing. You teach people. So certainly what I work on with one guy I'm not going to work on with the others. In Freddie's case, I'm trying to keep his swing shorter...in Stadler's case, his swing is too short. You apply some of the basic fundamentals to the person you're working with and see what happens."

Harmon admits that working with Touring professionals is a completely different experience from working with his members at River Oaks. "It can be tough to go spend a week with Lanny or Freddie or Steve Elkington and then come back home and work with a 40-handicap lady. But that's my job. It's difficult, but that's the life I've chosen."

He says it would not be hard to set up a career in which all he did was travel with the Tour and work with professional clients. But balanced against that is his desire for a home life for himself, his wife and four children. "I could do it," he says. "But I need the stability." Perhaps the nomadic lifestyle of the Claude Harmon family has something to do with Dick Harmon's desire for stability.

Still, there is no question that Claude Harmon's ability to evaluate a golf swing and fix what is wrong with it has passed down to the next generation.

Dick Harmon

The Practice Tee

I've never believed in instructing a student to purposely hit down on the ball or take a divot with the short or medium irons.

All golfers are built differently and can't be expected to swing the same way. Some women and senior players, for example, don't possess sufficient strength to pull the club powerfully into the ball on the downswing. Concentrating on swinging down can also breed swing flaws. All too often, a player thinking about taking a divot will become ball-bound, start the club back slowly and then jerk it down into impact, with body lunging toward the target. The results are bad balance, bad timing and bad shots.

A swing controlled by the big muscles will produce a sweeping blow. Allow your hands, arms and club to follow your torso as your body coils to the top of the swing, then unwinds into impact. Consciously "pulling" the club into the ball with the hands and arms relies on perfect timing for solid contact and is a mistake. Practice hitting short irons off a low tee to groove the sweeping swing.

Chapter Three

JIM McLEAN

THE QUEST FOR KNOWLEDGE

Some teachers are made and not born, and Jim
McLean is likely a member of that class. A skilled player of
the game—although not skilled enough to meet his goals
in that arena—McLean has spent most of a lifetime studying the great teachers of golf, taking lessons from them,
and teaching side-by-side with many. Through that experience, as well as his time on the practice range as both a
club professional and a teaching specialist, Jim McLean has
earned an informal Ph.D. in golf instruction.

McLean is a native of Seattle who literally grew up
on a golf course. Both his parents played and encouraged
him to take up the game at an early age, which he did. As
a result, he became a solid junior player. He traveled in
the circles of the other fine golfers from the Pacific
Northwest: Kermit Zarley, Babe Hiskey, and others. He
won the U.S. Junior and the Western Junior championships, which were enough to earn him a scholarship to

the University of Houston. A few years later, another Seattle youngster, Freddie Couples, would follow the same path to Houston.

The Cougars, as usual, had a load of talent on the team. McLean roomed with Bruce Lietzke and played with John Mahaffey and Bill Rogers. In fact, there were more than forty hopefuls in the giant program. Houston coach Dave Williams led his teams to seventeen national championships in his years at Houston and finished second numerous times.

Jim McLean was a star. He won three collegiate tournaments and was named All-American in 1972. During his collegiate career, he compiled an impressive amateur record, appearing in two U.S. Opens, making the cut in the Masters tournament, and winning the Pacific Coast Amateur at the Olympic Club in San Francisco, the Northwest Open, and three times the Northwest Amateur. "I thought I was gonna be a player," he says.

In 1974, McLean entered the PGA Tour's tough, six-day qualifying school and missed earning his Tour card by three shots. His roommate, Bruce Lietzke, missed by one. Bill Rogers made it. But this first failure was tougher on McLean that it probably should have been. "I just sort of burned out," he says. "I had been playing since age twelve and this tremendous pressure had built up inside. All of a sudden, I just felt like I wasn't having fun at something I loved to do."

Looking back, McLean now believes that one can divide tournament golf into four areas of expertise: the long game, the short game, the course management game, and the mental game, with each comprising twenty-five percent of the total player. McLean rates himself high in the first three categories and abysmally low in the last. "I had trouble with focus and in handling the pressures," he says. "When I went to the Tour school, I felt more intimidated than I should have. I didn't sleep well, and there were just a lot of other things that people don't understand. You talk to a Tour player and ask him which of my four elements is most important, and they'll all say the mental part."

Thus, McLean began to reassess his career plans. He knew Jack Burke, one of the owners (along with Jimmy Demeret) of the Champions Club in Houston, and called him for help. The two talked for several hours and the upshot was that McLean should pursue a club job, preferrably one for a while in the northeast because that way he would have winters off to sharpen his competitive game. He gave McLean three names to call—then urged him not to close the door on a pro career just yet.

McLean landed at the Westchester Country Club outside New York, working for its head professional Bob Watson. Watson was a well-connected pro in the New York metropolitan area who had served as president of the Met PGA section. The club had some 1,800 members, and McLean was thrown into its teaching programs. "I started teaching ladies clinics with Mary Lena Faulk," McLean recalls. "She was a good player and a great lady who had won several amateur events and then went pro and won

twenty-six times on the LPGA. She was a protege of
Harvey Penick. We had 120 ladies three times a week,
split into three groups of forty. Then I was put in charge
of the junior program in 1975."

Surprisingly, Jim McLean discovered that he loved
teaching. Perhaps there was an element of release from
the pressures of constantly preparing for and competing in
tournaments. The young pro thrived in his new environment. And he began to meet important people in the metropolitan area golf scene.

"I met Fran Sant'Angelo. Frannie knew everybody,
and he set me up with Ken Venturi," McLean says. "I went
out to Palm Springs in the winter of 1976 and worked
with Venturi."

Ken Venturi's career was just about out of gas by
then and he was set to begin his new career as a golf analyst for CBS. But he was also an effective teacher and
counted among his pupils a number of promising young
players. Venturi had worked under the tutelage of Byron
Nelson and had probably shot more rounds of golf with
Ben Hogan than anyone alive. "It was a tremendous experience to spend some serious quality time with Venturi that
winter," McLean recalls. "We played thirty-six holes a day,
had lunches and dinners together, just talking golf the
whole while."

After working hard on his game with Venturi,
McLean reentered the PGA Tour Qualifying School in
1977. In the preliminary tournament at the Bardmoor
Country Club in Tampa, he finished second to Mark

McCumber and qualified for the final grind in the six-round tournament at Pinehurst. He drove to the North Carolina town confident in himself and his game. But as he entered Pinehurst in a car with New York plates, he notes wryly, he was pulled over for speeding and hauled off to jail. McLean was eventually bailed out, but, he says today, the incident unnerved him. He shot 77 the first day and 73 the next to miss the first cut by a single stroke.

"It was like a message," McLean says. "This isn't going to work."

McLean was upended and upset again, and this time he was worried about his future. He spent that winter in Houston, consulting friends and fighting off panic. One of those friends, Bobby Walzel, informed him of a teacher named Jimmy Ballard who was promoting a radical approach in Alabama. McLean went to Pell City and enrolled in the Ballard school.

"I ended up paying to go through his school nine times," McLean laughs. "I found out that his so-called radical stuff wasn't so radical at all. But Ballard was at his peak then. Back in the late '70s, he was every bit as popular as David Leadbetter is today. You'd go down there, and everybody was going to him. Tour players and everyone else had to pay to go to Ballard's programs."

McLean was interested in why he had failed when the chips were down and what elements in the swings of other players helped them get through such situations. He studied Ballard's business operation and was influenced by

Ballard as a coach. "He was tremendously motivating as a coach, the first coach-like teacher I had ever seen," McLean says. "I watched how he ran a school and how he handled the people who came through."

Suddenly, McLean found himself hooked on learning about learning. He wanted to be around teachers and watch what they were doing. After spending weeks with Jimmy Ballard, he continued down to Florida and settled at Frenchman's Creek Golf Club in Palm Beach. There he found three great teachers: Gardner Dickenson, Tony Penna, and Jack Grout, who had his famous pupil, Jack Nicklaus, on the practice tee. "I was there every day," McLean recalls. "I played with Gardner almost every day and talked to him a lot. I talked to Penna, who was very interesting. And I took lessons from Jack Grout and watched him work with Nicklaus. I would just kinda sit there and watch what they were doing."

Florida was always a hotbed of winter golf with Tour players visiting teachers, other pros running golf school operations, and hordes of tourists flocking to the warm sunshine for both golf and golf instruction. McLean traveled around the state visiting teachers and programs, in part to work on and learn more about his own game and in part to watch teachers teaching. McLean also visited a few of the then newly organized Golf Digest Schools and spent time with Bob Toski, who had been in charge of organizing that program. He also spent time with Paul

Runyan, a teacher who had played with the great Johnny Revolta.

Then, when he heard about an instructor employing unusual techniques in Phoenix, he went there to meet the man, Joe Nichols. "He was a brilliant teacher," McLean says, "one of the greatest with the average golfer I ever saw. He worked at a little ranch in Phoenix with an executive course and a range and was booked solid for months in advance. He worked with Tom Purtzer, Mike Morley, Howard Twitty, and others and did some really different stuff. He used something called a rotar, which was about leveraging the club up and rotaring it around— really different."

In the winters McLean was a golfing nomad, following the sun in search of the answers or at least watching others attempt to provide them to their students. But in the summers he always went back to New York and his club job at Westchester, networking his way up the ladder. In 1979, he was hired as head golf professional at Scarsdale's Sunningdale Club, another first-rate club in the New York area. It was a pivotal step for McLean, fulfilling one of his early goals to be the head professional at a prestigious club.

His head pro job gave McLean a base. He had a firm foundation in spring, summer, and fall, where he taught golf, operated his pro shop, and made even more friends and contacts in the big-money world of metropolitan New York. He also had the freedom to play competitive tournaments in the metro area, with the PGA section there; and in the winters, with his club closed for the season, he could spend three or four months in the warmth of Florida and Arizona, both playing tournament golf and continuing his quest to observe and pick the brains of the great teachers.

McLean had met the incomparable Claude Harmon, longtime head professional at Winged Foot, the year just before Harmon retired. But McLean accepted a winter job one year at the Morningside Club in Palm Springs, across the street from Tamarisk, where Harmon wintered. That year, the last before Harmon died, the two men became close. They scheduled a weekly lunch appointment where Harmon would spin his legendary tales.

Another New York connection was with Harry "Lighthorse" Cooper, a legendary professional from the early days of the PGA Tour who taught at Westchester late in his life. Cooper had played in the era of Walter Hagen and Bobby Jones and had worked with Ben Hogan. "When I was at Westchester, he was out there on the range with me every day," McLean says. "I took a lot of lessons from him. He had certain swing positions that he believed in and would teach."

When Jim McLean arrived at Sunningdale, he'd already worked with and for some of the most notable players and teachers of his age. He immediately put this to good use, setting up a program for junior golfers and initiating work with promising players.

One player with whom he began working at Westchester was George Zahringer, one of the finest amateur golfers in the country at the time. Zahringer was a well-known name only in amateur golf circles and mainly in the northeastern United States. He was named Player of the Decade in the PGA's Metro section in 1980, after a decade in which he dominated tournaments in the area. He qualified for the U.S. Amateur nine years in a row and went to the final sixteen three times. He won four consecutive Met Amateurs and six in all in the 1980s. He also scored big in the Met Open, winning once and otherwise always finishing in the top ten, even against fields that included the likes of Jim Albus, Larry Laoretti, Dick Siderowf, and other accomplished players from metropolitan New York and upper New Jersey. But Zahringer was only a six-month golfer. In the winter, when the pros went south for their jobs, Zahringer would put his clubs away and return to his job, for Bear, Stearns on Wall Street, and his family.

"What I did with George was give him a Bruce Lietzke game," McLean recalls. "When I first started working with him in 1975, he was a strong handicapper, about a five, but he hooked the ball. And because, like Bruce, he didn't want to play that much, I gave him a game that he didn't have to work very hard on. And for him, and Lietzke for that matter, that meant hitting a fade with every shot instead."

Zahringer's fade game propelled him into the record books of the Met Section and helped McLean as well. In 1989 the two qualified for the finals of the national Skins Game pro-am, held the day before the famous Thanksgiving weekend Skins Game, and they won. The check for the professional McLean was $61,000.

Another success story for McLean was Billy Britton, a journeyman PGA Tour player from Staten Island. Britton had played on the Tour for five years before losing his playing card by failing to win enough money. He had been out of golf for a year when he realized that if he was able to regain his playing card, go back on Tour and make fifteen cuts, he would qualify for a pension.

"Billy is a great guy, but he didn't have a lot of confidence," McLean says. "We decided to make some big changes, both in the way he thought about the swing and what he was trying to do in his game."

Britton requalified for the Tour in 1987 but lost his card again after that year. Finally, in 1988 he regained his card—for good. And in 1989 he won a tournament, the Centel Classic. Britton finished thirty-fourth on the money list in 1989 and won more than $1 million over the next four years. He not only gained his pension, he became a good player again. "It's really fun to take someone, help him make big changes, and have him go back and win again," McLean says.

As McLean got deeper and deeper into his teaching career, he found that he was becoming a better player himself. He won tournaments in the Met Section of the

PGA of America, played in fourteen national club pro events, and participated in other tournaments sponsored by the Florida PGA of America sections. "I wanted to continue to play the game," McLean says. "You don't have to be a good player to teach the game, but especially when you're working with PGA Tour players, it helps that they know I've been there, that I've had the gun to my head. I know what it feels like, I know what it's like not to be able to breathe."

And Jim McLean always seized opportunities to observe great golfers, chat with them, and expand his knowledge of the game. He spent time with Byron Nelson. One winter in Orlando he watched Sam Snead play golf with Roberto deVicenzo for several weeks. "In the days before the Senior Tour, they used to go out and play a lot," he recalls. "I think sometimes there were just two of us watching them. I'd just hang out with them, walk eighteen holes, and watch. I didn't even talk to Sam that much, but I spent some time with Roberto and learned some things."

The one teacher who influenced McLean more than any other was Carl Welty. Welty is today director of instruction at the La Costa Resort in Southern California, home of the PGA Tour's Mercedes Tournament of Champions. But McLean first met Welty when he was an assistant pro at an undersized nine-hole course in Seattle. Welty had tutored under Paul Runyon and was good friends with Gene Littler, Chuck Courtney, Bill Rogers, and others. Back in the 1960s Welty had begun filming the swings of his professional friends, using the era's primitive eight-mm cameras.

"He had a great film library," McLean says. "He used to film everybody's swing, including mine as a junior player! He had a thirst for knowledge about the golf swing that was unsurpassed."

Welty worked with the young McLean and helped him win the Washington State Junior title, which forged a lifelong friendship. Today, McLean visits La Costa every year for the Tournament of Champions. He stays with Welty, and, what else, the two talk golf. Welty's library—he was one of the first to use videotape in his lessons—is still one of the most comprehensive compilations of golf swings. Many of the touring pros who play in the LaCosta event stop in for several days to consult with Welty. "Anytime I see some new idea or theory, I always call Carl and run it by him," McLean says. "He really looks at what works on Tour. He keeps detailed statistics to help identify the best ball strikers and the worst, and he studies the differences."

That kind of intellectual curiousity and attention to detail is what characterizes the Jim McLean Golf Schools of today. Operating at the Doral Golf Learning Center at the Doral resort in Miami, McLean assigns each of his teaching assistants to take a piece of video of a Tour player and to study one part of the body. "One guy takes the right knee and finds out what it is doing. Another takes the left knee. Someone else might look at the left foot—is it on the ground? Is the right foot twisting at impact? How many players do one thing, how many another? It's all research. And if you don't do the research, you don't have much to teach," he says.

And what has he divined from his research? McLean defers to a comment that Johnny Miller once made to him: "A swing that produces quality golf shots under pressure is a great swing, no matter what it looks like." That's why the peculiar swings of a Ray Floyd, Nancy Lopez, or Lee Trevino cannot be discounted or disqualified, he says.

"I'm much more in a player's mode," McLean says. "I've studied the physics of the golf swing as much as anybody else, but I'm also aware that there are a lot of things that can work. *Golf Magazine*, which I occasionally contribute to, recently ran a cover article that asked the question 'Should You Change Your Swing?' And the answer they gave was no, just learn to live with what you've got and adapt around it. Well, that's completely wrong. We change people's swings all the time."

What it comes down to, McLean believes, is that a teacher is judged not by the breadth of his knowledge, the quality of his equipment, or how broad his vocabulary is. A teacher is judged solely on whether his golfers improve at the game. "Look at Harvey Penick," McLean says. "He didn't say much when he was giving lessons, but what he did say were pearls of wisdom . . . brilliant things. It worked because he cared about the people he worked with, and that made him one of the greatest teachers ever."

Still, today's marketplace demands technological innovation, and McLean goes with the flow. At his school at Doral, he has helped devise what he calls "The Superstation," an indoor video studio that can capture a golf swing from four different angles with playback and split screen and all the other whiz-bang gimmickry available today.

Still, McLean views videotape with guarded optimism. "I think the experience I've had in using video has taught me to be very careful with it. It's still the greatest teaching device, and I use it every day, but it has to be a sharing experience. The student has to be involved in the process. And I've watched so many great teachers help a student get better in a half hour without videotape—and do that consistently, day after day—to know that video is not the total answer."

For McLean, just as important as playback on a video machine is a teacher's gut instinct and the ability to draw out a student's needs. Watching the golf swing and knowing what needs fixing, controlling how much information is fed to the student, and understanding what that golfer thinks and feels all make a difference in teaching.

Learning about teaching in general has been Jim McLean's lifelong pursuit. He has studied at the Performance Enhancement Institute at West Point, he has dissected the practices of football coaches like Bruce Coslet of the New York Jets, and he has read the works of Bobby Knight and Pat Riley.

"The way we've organized our schools is based on the realization that we're in the teaching and learning business," McLean says. "And having great facilities and good golf courses and access to fine resorts are important, but they're just a part of the overall picture: Good teachers are generally interesting people, good communicators, and have an enthusiasm for the game."

In recent years McLean's prominence as a golf instructor has swelled. When the KSL Recreation Corporation purchased the Doral resort several years ago, it was impressed with his facility and his numbers; he was putting people in the hotel. As a result, the company named him director of golf instruction and asked him to design a new practice and teaching facility at its other resort property: PGA West and the LaQuinta resort in Palm Springs. This expansive new facility is one of the best in the world and is home to a Dave Pelz short-game school as well as a David Leadbetter golf academy. McLean is also setting up the golf instructional facility for the new Chelsea Piers project in New York. Four former shipping piers on the Hudson River are being transformed into a four-season sports complex that will include a trilevel golf practice range.

McLean continues to work from time to time with touring professionals. Their problems, of course, require quite a different approach. "Tour players are very knowledgeable," he says. "They know what's going on, and they operate at a totally different level. They're the finest players in the world, and they want to talk about the trajectory of their ball flight and the spin rates and other aspects of the game that most people don't get into. And Tour players are working with the mental part of the game, visualization and the higher elements of the game. It's stimulating to work with them and fun, especially when they do well!"

McLean has had his share of success stories with Tour players. In addition to the rebirth of Billy Britton's game, McLean worked with Tom Kite in 1992. Kite had had a rare off year in 1991. At the Tournament of Champions event in January 1992, McLean tutored Kite for five days. Later in the season, when the Tour visited Miami for the Doral Ryder Open, the two spent another week together on the range, using the swing computers, video, and other hightech equipment. McLean visited Kite in Houston for more tune-ups. That summer Kite ended a slump by winning the BellSouth Classic in Atlanta, followed a week later by the U.S. Open crown at Pebble Beach. "He and Ben Crenshaw flew back to New York together after the Open," McLean recalls, "and we all went out to dinner to celebrate. It was a special night."

Kite, of course, was a longtime student of Harvey Penick and also works with Chuck Cooke in Austin, Texas. But McLean, who used to play college golf against Texan Kite, considers him a good friend as well as a client.

McLean says he gave Peter Jacobsen a talking to at the Tournament of Champions in 1993 after Jacobsen had abandoned the Tour for a job as color analyst for NBC. "I told him I just hated to see Peter Jacobsen go out of the game at age thirty-eight, when he'd been such a great ball striker," McLean recalls. "I encouraged him to get out of the tower and get back to work on his game and told him he could win again." To that end, Jacobsen visited McLean at Doral, where he also fine-tuned his short game with Dave Pelz. Jacobsen remotivated himself and returned to the Tour, winning two tournaments in 1995 and performing on the '95 Ryder Cup team.

McLean has also worked with Brad Faxon. "He came to see me at Sleepy Hollow in 1991," McLean says. "He had worked with several other guys and was just kind of scratching the ball around. We developed a long relationship. He stayed in my house, and I'd go to the Tour stops and work with him. It was fun to see 'Fax' pull his game together, work on a lot of things, and see him develop into the fine player that he is today." In 1990, Faxon had won just $197,000. The next year, working with McLean, he jumped to thirty-fourth on the money list, winning more than $422,000. In 1992, he earned $812,000.

"It's fun to work with those guys, to visit with them, and there's certainly an element of notoriety and publicity when you're working with Tour players," McLean says. "I feel like I had a little something to do with some of these guys' successes, but in the end they're the ones who have to go out there and hit the shots."

McLean's many successes with Tour players is just one page from the larger story of his career, a career in which he made the transition from club professional to noted teacher of the game. And, he notes, that's a path rarely followed these days.

"Teaching is the biggest thing that changed since I got in the PGA of America," McLean says. "Most guys stopped teaching when they got to be a head professional. Many turn that aspect over to their assistants. And the business has changed. It used to be that one could barely get by teaching golf, while today it's a huge business."

Americans crave improvement, McLean has found. And he has developed a system and teaching environment that helps America's golfers improve. McLean's goal is to educate his students enough about the game and their golf swing so they can analyze their own problems and know how to correct them. He also encourages his students to go back home and continue to take lessons from their local pros.

For Jim McLean, studying the golf swing has been a lifelong quest. It's a journey that has not yet ended and likely never will.

JIM McLEAN

PRACTICE TEE

In every lesson I give, I try to analyze why a particular student is having trouble with his game. I always look at all four main areas of the game: the long game, the short game, the mental/emotional game, and the management game. Once I narrow in on the problem area, I'll focus the lesson on this aspect of the game.

It is very important that each student has a crystal clear picture of what is currently happening. It is my responsibility to deliver this information to them.

When I look at a golf swing, I break it down. I look at the body action separately. Then I look at what the club is doing, again, separately. Isolating these two basic actions of the total swing helps me establish an accurate diagnosis.

With each of these two main parts of the swing, I look at eight checkpoint steps on the video. At each of these steps I look at corridors of acceptability and whether the student stays within these ranges.

My longtime work with Carl Welty (director of instruction at La Costa) has given me a solid understanding of golf's true fundamentals and the understanding that there are many allowable differences in great golf swings.

Chapter Four

DAVE PELZ

RESEARCHING THE SHORT GAME

Dave Pelz became a golf teacher because he couldn't beat Jack Nicklaus.

Of course, if every good golfer who ever lost to Nicklaus had turned into an instructor, there would be a surplus of teachers numbering in the thousands. But it is true that many club professionals and golf teachers turned to that line of work after coming to the realization at some point in their careers that they didn't have the game to compete on the Tour. For Pelz that realization came when as a collegiate golfer at the University of Indiana he compiled a perfect record against Ohio State's young blond star: Pelz was 0-22 in matches against Nicklaus.

Dave Pelz grew up in Lexington, Kentucky. His father, a district manager with Nabisco, was a good golfer who used to take the young Pelz to the golf course while he played and leave the youngster on the putting green.

Pelz remembers spending hours on the green fooling around waiting for his Dad to get through. Later Pelz caddied for his father.

As a result, he became a good player at a young age. Pelz remembers playing in his first match at seven. He doesn't recall who won, but it was against a seventy-seven-year-old man, and the unusual circumstances of the game attracted the attention of the local newspaper, which sent a photographer to shoot the odd duo.

"I don't remember who won," Pelz says. "I think we probably fired about 150 at each other! But I got my picture in the newspaper—a little seven-year-old and the seventy-seven-year-old man. I thought getting my picture in the sports pages at age seven was pretty special. I've been a golf nut ever since."

Because of his father's job, Pelz lived all over the Midwest. He played high school golf first in Youngstown, Ohio, and then moved to Cleveland. It was when he began playing in state junior events that he first ran into the chubby youngster from Columbus. Nicklaus, Pelz recalls, would eventually win everything: the Ohio State Amateur, the State Open, and more.

Although today Pelz is a big man at well over six feet, in high school he played guard on the basketball team, his second love in sports. After being named to the All-Greater Cleveland conference team, Pelz was offered a basketball scholarship to college but decided instead to take the golf scholarship Indiana offered him.

"I was just good enough to get the scholarship from a Big Ten school," Pelz remembers. "I was excited and took it because golf was my first love. I was an okay basketball player, except that I couldn't run and jump! Typical white man's disease. I could shoot, but not like Larry Bird."

At Indiana, Pelz and his teammates competed regularly against Nicklaus and Ohio State. Head to head, home and away, round robins, stroke play, match play—Nicklaus always came out ahead. Pelz remembers one event where he did manage to win a point from Nicklaus. It was in a thirty-six-hole event: in the morning match, Pelz shot 72 to Nicklaus' 74 and won the point.

"In the afternoon round, I'll never forget shaking hands with him at the start. He looked at me and said 'Good luck,' and I thought to myself 'You'd better be ready...this guy is not happy!'" Pelz played his heart out that afternoon, turning in a 73. Nicklaus fired a cool 64 and won the last two points.

"Jack Nicklaus is the reason I did not turn professional when I got out of college," Pelz says flatly. "I thought to myself if I can't beat this kid, what am I going to do against real pros? Of course, I didn't know how good he was or what he was going to become."

Being unable to defeat the kid from Ohio made Pelz reassess his career choices; luckily he had an education to fall back on. Pelz had majored in physics at Indiana with minors in mathematics and philosophy. He was a numbers-oriented person who enjoyed mathematic formulas and scientific principles.

He landed a job at the Goddard Space Flight Research Center outside Washington D.C. It was the 1960s and the Golden Age of the space race; the United States and Soviet Union competed to see who could be first to land a man on the moon and explore the outer reaches of space.

Pelz immersed himself in his new career, working on orbital projects for Venus and Mars, traveling the world, and conducting lab research. He got married, started a family, and seemed to have found an exciting niche for himself.

And he quit golf. Completely. His job chewed up almost all his time, and when the children were born, that meant even more demands. And, Pelz discovered, there were not many good public golf courses in the suburban Washington area; the one he had tried to play was so crowded that one had to arrive at 4 a.m. to get a tee time for 10:30. And all that just to play a five-hour round on a poorly maintained course! So, Pelz put his clubs in the closet and abandoned the game for several years.

But as with most good golfers, there is a strong competitive gene in the pool, and Pelz needed an outlet for his. Improbably, he turned to racecar driving. After getting a license from the Sports Car Association of America, Pelz built a Jaguar and entered races at Watkins Glen, Virginia International Raceway, Marlboro, and elsewhere.

"Driving a racecar sounds exciting, but you have to understand, I'm neither a rich guy nor a nut case," Pelz says. "So I told myself I'd drive as fast as I could, but I wouldn't really push it all the way."

In his first year of racing, adopting a conservative approach, he finished every race but always well back in the pack. In the next season, armed with increasing confidence, he began pushing a little harder, drifting into high speed turns, taking the more aggressive line, and trying to wring more speed from his car. "As I got better, I started losing control of my emotions," he remembers. "I started really racing, driving as fast as I could, and taking every chance I encountered."

With a more aggressive approach came crashes. His first occured at Marlboro when he entered a hairpin, jammed the accelerator down, locked up, and went into the wall at about 80 mph. "I kinda messed up my car," Pelz remembers.

Six months later at Watkins Glen, Pelz had his second, and last, crash. At the end of a straightaway, doing about 150 mph, he touched the brakes and nothing happened. He flew off the end of the racecourse and into trees. Dodging the hardwood, he turned off the ignition and downshifted into third gear, slowing to about 80, then in a second to 60 mph. Finally he plowed into a wire fence, which wrapped the car up and stopped it. "I survived," Pelz says simply, "and I never raced again. I realized that in golf, you can have a bad day, shoot 80, and go home disgusted. But the next morning you can wake up and try again. In racing, you have a bad day, and you're dead. I had great luck with two potentially fatal accidents, but I knew they were happening because I had started using the entire track and pushing the envelope out further and further. And my wife was pregnant. So I quit and never looked back. I am a golfer, not a racer."

Pelz returned to the links, joining a private club. He worked at Goddard for sixteen years, focusing on myriad esoteric research projects on space. By his tenth year, he was a senior scientist with a crew of twenty-five working in a laboratory he directed. He was named by NASA a principal investigator, in charge of devising and testing experimental efforts. He designed experimental products, had them built by contractors around the country, put them on satellites, assembled and analyzed the data, and wrote technical articles. "It was a neat job in that nobody really knew exactly what we were doing, and thus nobody could check up on us!" Pelz laughs. "It was pure science, which, although there may not have been immediate practical applications, eventually yielded tremendous spin-offs in terms of scientific knowledge and product developments." Pelz also learned how to manipulate computer-generated data to perform sophisticated modeling and analysis.

As his career developed, his golf game reawakened as well. His handicap dropped quickly to zero and stayed there. He won his club championship year after year and began competing in other local amateur events. He even entered national tournaments, but his unimpressive results stirred those old insecurities about his ability to compete nationally. "I would win the club tournament easily, but go to a national tournament and I'd shoot 75 and finish in the middle of the pack," Pelz says.

After several years of such results, Pelz the scientist decided to make a research study of Pelz the golfer. Examining his career, one quick conclusion was evident: Pelz was not a good putter and never had been. He knew that he was a good ball striker, but he had never putted the ball well enough to reach the top level.

"Looking back, I could see that I always lost it on the greens," he says. "There were times when I hit more fairways than Jack, hit more greens, did all the things that I thought I would need to win, and he'd beat me because he could putt better. So I made a project out of finding out what it took to putt."

Pelz turned to his scientific training and years of experience working at Goddard and on NASA projects. Just as he had to devise experiments to help scientists answer questions about Venus or Mars, now he devised experiments aimed at solving the mystery of putting. He created measurable tests and worked on the project nights and weekends over several years. The scientific method is a slow and careful one.

Finally Pelz devised a test that could accurately measure some of the elements in putting, centrally aim and speed. He ran the tests on himself and was amazed at what he learned.

"I had never realized it, but I discovered I was hitting every putt on the toe of the putter," he says. "So every putt I hit would be slightly to the right of the target and have slightly less energy than it should have."

Pelz's tests showed that if a golfer faces a right-to-left breaking putt, hits the ball on the toe, and starts it to the right of the proper line, in many cases the ball will not have the correct speed (or energy), so it will break too much and often go into the hole—kind of a self-correcting mistake. But on left-to-right breakers, the ball starts below the proper line, and with its lack of speed, breaks away from the hole and misses. "And I'd known for twenty years that I couldn't make left-to-right putts," Pelz says. "But I'd never known why. All of a sudden, knowing why, I fixed it."

He created a practice aid that helped him learn to hit the ball on the sweet spot instead of the toe, and it worked. His left-to-right putts began dropping regularly. "And for a scratch amateur, that's big," he says. "That's about half your putts. A big difference."

Suddenly, Pelz qualified for his first U.S. Amateur, and in the local tournament for the U.S. Open, plus he began shooting par or better in other major tournaments. "I had always concluded that I just didn't have the heart or the courage or whatever it is that champions have," Pelz says. "And while looking back now I feel I still had no chance of being a great player, I felt at the time that this was really impressive and fun. Bad putters are always bad

putters, and great putters are always great. You don't usually change groups. But I did it."

Having put his scientific theories to practical use on
himself, Pelz began to ask, what next? If he could correct
his own flaws, could he also look at another's putting
methods, pinpoint problems areas, and correct those as
well? His golfing friends, noting his improved putting,
began to ask him for help.

Finally, a group of D.C. businessmen made Pelz a
proposition. They wanted to start a golf company to man-
ufacture and market Pelz' expertise and to sell his practice
aids and putters. "I was going to stay at Goddard, but be
president of this new golf equipment company and
become a multimillionaire," Pelz says. "That's what they
told me."

In September 1974, his company began manufacturing the Teacher Putter. It had twin prongs that could be
affixed to the face of the club for practice. The prongs
were spaced just far enough apart to frame the putter's
sweet spot for the width of a golf ball. With practice, one
could learn to stroke the ball on that all-important sweet
spot every time. For play, the prongs could be moved
around to the back of the putter and used as visual aids.

Unfortunately, Pelz's patented design for the original Teacher Putter was ruled illegal by the U.S. Golf
Association, which said it was "designed to be adjustable
during play," even though only an idiot would actually
choose to putt during a round with the prongs projecting

forward off the face, because even a slight mishit would send the ball skittering off line. Still, Pelz reworked the product to make it conform.

That run-in with golf's ruling body—not Pelz's last—was just one early problem with his new company. He was still working ten hours a day at Goddard, struggling to keep his performance from slipping. Yet he realized that being in the golf business would consume more time and energy than he thought. He wanted to attend the Masters, the U.S. Open, and other tournaments and talk golf with players and do more research on putting.

Finally, he approached his supervisor at Goddard and explained the problem. He was given a year's leave of absence with no loss of benefits or seniority. His employers thought a year in the real world of business would be good experience for Pelz, so they let him go and said he'd be welcome back at the end of the year. "It was a wonderful thing," he says. "I changed careers without risk and I also started my new career at the top, not the bottom."

Perhaps he should have started at the bottom, because Dave Pelz turned out to be a horrible businessman. His investors had raised $75,000 for the new enterprise; at the end of the first year, it was all gone. The company made the Teacher Putters but had ineffective, almost non-existent, distribution to the marketplace. Pelz spent around $50,000 for a single ad in *Golf Digest* that generated interest in the golf community, but the product was largely unavailable. Golfers would see the ad, then go to their local pro shops to purchase one. But the professionals would shrug their shoulders and say "never heard of it!"

Then came the problems with the USGA, which called for a major retooling of the putter. Pelz focused more on putting greens, measuring angles and speed as clubface met ball than on profit and loss statements. "I conducted things horribly that first year," he says, "but at the end of the year I was convinced I was a golfer trained in physics rather than a physicist who was a golfer. I loved every minute of that year and said 'If I can enjoy it this much losing money, think about how much fun it would be to make money!'"

So, Dave Pelz resigned from Goddard Space Center. He mortgaged his home and scraped together about $40,000 to bankroll year two. At the end of that year, his accountant told him he had lost $42,000 and was in serious financial trouble.

But Pelz had made some inroads with touring professionals on the PGA Tour. They, too, experienced immediate and positive results from using Pelz's Teaching Putter. He had also developed other measurement devices to provide factual feedback on what was going on with the putting stroke. Pelz's stuff worked, and six touring pros told him to keep going; they'd help with his expenses in the third year. "In my third year, I lost all their money," Pelz says. "It was around $24,000. So now I'd lost $75,000,

$42,000, and $24,000 in three years. Now as a mathematician, I look at that as an indication that at least I was doing better every year. Of course, my accountant had another view. He said I was bankrupt, had lost all my benefits with the government, and was in danger of losing the house, the cars. He told me to get out and go back to Goddard and beg. But I'm very stubborn and said 'I'm not bankrupt if your creditors don't make you pay.'"

So Pelz made the rounds of all those to whom he owed money and said "Don't worry, I'll pay you back." He rounded up yet another group of brave investors and in his fourth year nearly broke even. In year five, the company actually made a small profit. In 1982, Pelz moved the company to Austin, Texas, taking advantage of the year-round warm weather. That year he introduced his controversial Three-Ball Putters. These unusual looking clubs had long faces with three plastic orbs in the shape and size of golf balls attached end to end and finished off with a smaller end plate. The club's purpose was to help the golfer in aim and alignment on the green. Again, the USGA's club-conformity rules makers intervened, forcing Pelz to spend a couple of years trying to develop a model that conformed.

Finally scratching out a living, Pelz made what he calls his best move: he exited the club manufacturing business. A consultant told him that his strength was in teaching and doing research and testing, but that every dollar he was making in those areas was being sunk into the manufacturing business, which had to go up against the big club makers and their larger marketing machines.

Since the mid-1980s, Pelz concentrated on the short game at both the research and teaching levels. Today he is considered the leading expert in the short game, putting, and chipping. Dozens of top professionals on the PGA, LPGA, and Nike Tours consult him, and he now operates the successful Dave Pelz Short Game School at the Boca Raton Resort and Club and at PGA West in La Quinta, California.

Free to conduct scientific research on the short game, Pelz has contributed much to the science of putting a golf ball into the hole. In his book, *Putt Like the Pros*, Pelz relates his early attempts to build a perfect putting device that would enable him to scientifically measure putting data. When an early version lost a putt-out with the late Bert Yancey, at the time considered one of the PGA Tour's best putters, Pelz went back to the drawing board.

Pelz eventually developed the True Roller, a ramp-like device not unlike the Stimpmeter that is used to measure green speeds. The True Roller gives Pelz the ability to control aim and speed with highly calibrated precision. Still, Pelz found that even the True Roller missed a good percentage of putts, which led him to further study of both the ball and the putting surface.

Widely known is the story of perfectionist Ben Hogan, who carried a metal circle in his pocket, which he used to measure the roundness of each new ball he unwrapped. Pelz, too, learned that not every ball is manufactured to perfect specifications. By using a spin test on balls floating in a solution of water and Epson salts, Pelz discovered that some balls are also weighted unevenly to one side or the other, which can affect how they roll on a putting green. While only perfectionists might be expected to spend an hour spinning balls in water to find which ones are precisely balanced, Pelz's studies show that an unbalanced ball can deviate over the course of a putt by an inch or more; a startling statistic that could provide a major reason for many missed putts.

Pelz's compulsive search for quantifiable answers also led him to study putting greens. He learned, with his unerring True Roller device, that more putts would fall in the hole in the early morning on freshly mowed, untracked greens. In late afternoon conditions, on greens filled with footprints and spike marks, even the True Roller could only make roughly thirty percent of the putts. More study led to Pelz's theory of the lumpy doughnut hole.

Most golfers know enough etiquette to avoid stepping directly on the hole. In fact, Pelz found that most golfers bending over to pluck their ball out of the hole step eighteen inches from the cup. In the course of a day's play, that creates a "lumpy doughnut hole" of footprints around the cup, in effect creating a minute circular ridge around the hole. Thus, Pelz believes, to make a greater percentage of putts, one must putt the ball hard enough to get a slowing ball up and over the doughnut-hole ramp. That is why he tells his golf school clients that the perfect putt speed is one in which the ball goes eighteen inches past the cup.

In the wedge and chip game, Pelz's research has been equally exhaustive. He has identified five positions in the backswing and throughswing and has students swing the club to these numbered stations to execute the desired shot.

To those who consider golf more of an art than a science, Dave Pelz can be annoying as he tries to reduce the basics of the game to formulaic precision. For most golfers, a ten-point putter performance test, which requires hitting one-hundred putts with each of two putters from varying distances and breaks and keeping careful tabulations of the results, goes way beyond the pale of trying to become a better putter. Yet, at the same time, for Pelz's professional clients, and for those who are deadly earnest about becoming better short game players and putters, there is almost nothing that is too time consuming or boring to effect such a result.

Pelz relates the story of a session early in his career with Tom Kite, a noted grinder. At the time, Pelz was talking in somewhat vague terms. He'd say something like "I'd like you to keep the putter blade square to the target line through impact and keep the path close to the target line throughout the swing." To which Tom Kite replied "How square? How much face-angle rotation is in the perfect stroke? How much, exactly, should I bring the putter path inside the target line? Don't tell me 'a little more' or 'a little less' of something. Tell me exactly what the perfect stroke is, and I'll develop it!"

With the precision of a trained physicist, Pelz has spent his career searching for the answer to those questions. His body of work on the short game is matchless in its scope and depth. No one on the planet, this one at least, knows more about putting and pitching than Dave Pelz.

That explains why professional clients, such as Peter Jacobsen, who worked for several weeks with Pelz in the fall of 1994 before winning two PGA tournaments in early 1995, flock to his teaching facilities in Boca Raton and La Quinta. At last count, Pelz has worked with twenty-nine players from the PGA Tour, twenty-three from the LPGA, and fourteen from the European Tour. But it is equally true that ordinary hackers flock to Pelz, selling out his three- and five-day short game schools with regularity.

Pelz thinks he knows why. "At most schools students leave hitting the ball better, but that's not scoring better," he says. "Our students score better, not because we're great teachers but because we're working on the part of the game where most of the strokes are lost. Eighty percent of handicaps occur in the short game, and that's where we help."

Ever the scientist, Pelz even knows by how much. His follow-up tracking shows that his average student improves his handicap by 3.8 shots within a year after attending a Pelz school. That's a statistic that's attention-getting for a golfer from any part of the galaxy.

DAVE PELZ

PRACTICE TEE

Putting stances and styles vary greatly in golf—there is no right way or wrong way. However, one setup characteristic that a great many excellent putters on the PGA Tour employ and that I consider crucial is that their shoulders are aimed parallel to the target line.

Examining your shoulder alignment outdoors is something that can be done quite easily at the practice green. All you need is a friend, your putter and two other golf clubs.

Find as straight a putt as possible. Set up to the putt and have your friend lay one club along the line to the hole, just to one side of the ball. Then ask him or her to place the second club along the inside of your shoulders and hold the club steady in that position.

Step away and check if your shoulder line (as represented by the club your friend is holding) runs parallel to the left of the target line (represented by the club on the ground). If it does, great. If not, have your friend "direct" you toward the correct parallel-left shoulder position.

Learning the look and feel of the parallel-left shoulder position is a big step toward developing an arm stroke that requires no special manipulations.

—From *Putt Like The Pros* by Dave Pelz, Harper Collins, 1989.

Chapter Five

JIM FLICK

A TEACHER'S LIFE

Jim Flick was startled by a simple question. He was driving with his wife to the airport in Phoenix to fly to the PGA Teaching Summit, the annual confab of teaching pros, where he would deliver an address at a seminar entitled "How To Be A Master Teacher." In the car, his wife asked what he was going to talk about. When he told her the topic, she asked, "What's a master teacher? I've never seen that explained anywhere."

His wife's question got Flick to thinking. He thought he knew what a master teacher was—he had the notes and a list in his briefcase to back it up. But he had to agree that *his* definition and criteria might not be someone else's, especially if the one making the decision was an unhappy golf student. He delivered his address, but he amended it somewhat. "There have been," he told the other golf instructors at the seminar, "only nine or ten master teachers in the history of the game. And I ain't one of 'em."

Flick was being overly modest. If a master teacher is one who has persevered at his craft for many years, has worked successfully with both the greats and the nobodies of the game, has made a lot friends along the way, and yet is still searching for ways to become a better teacher, then Jim Flick is a master.

Flick grew up in Bedford, Indiana. His father, who worked for the electric company, had been a fine player as a young man in French Lick. In fact, the elder Flick had been a caddie for Gene Sarazen when the PGA Championship was played at the French Lick Golf Club in 1924.

That long-standing interest in the game was passed down from father to son. Flick was an all-around athlete who excelled in many sports, but his father always kept his son's ego in check. He recalls that when he was in junior high school, the local newspaper praised his exploits after a good performance in a basketball game. "My father told me to read it, enjoy it, and then forget about it," he says. "He told me, 'You're living in Bedford, Indiana, which is an awfully small part of the world. And the only thing that newspaper had to write about today was that junior high school basketball game, which in the general scope of things is not very important.' He told me never to base my self-esteem on something so insignificant."

Flick's athletic prowess enabled him to capture a scholarship to Wake Forest University, but as a basketball player, not a golfer. When he arrived at Wake Forest, he

joined the golf team, which included one Arnold Palmer
from Latrobe, Pennsylvania. In part because of Arnie's
influence and Flick's own love for the game, he soon
switched from basketball to golf. As a sophomore, he was
a scratch player but could only qualify for the second
string, although he did letter with the varsity his last two
years.

One autumn, Flick, Palmer, and their roommates,
all members of the golf team, were selling tickets at the
Wake Forest football game, a way scholarship students
could earn a little extra cash. Flick and Palmer had trouble balancing the cash receipts, so their buddies decided
to leave without them and head over to Duke for a
dance that night. On the road, the car swerved and
crashed, killing both young men. Palmer and Flick
became roommates after the accident, but Arnold was so
distraught by the death of his friend Buddy Worsham that
he eventually left Wake Forest and joined the coast
guard.

After college, Flick served in the armed forces during the Korean War then tried his hand on the PGA Tour
for a few seasons. "I found out that my talent level as a
player did not warrant my staying out there," he says
today. The same, of course, could not be said of his former roommate, who went on to glory and golf history.

Flick became a club professional instead. His first
job was as teaching assistant at Evansville Country Club in
Evansville, Indiana. From there he moved to the
Connersville (Indiana) Country Club for five years, then to

Losantiville Country Club in a Cincinnati suburb, where he spent sixteen contented years. In addition to his head professional duties, he found a membership receptive to lessons.

In Cincinnati he tutored several young golfers destined for golfing glory. One of his early students was Susie Maxwell Berning, who won the U.S. Women's Open three times (in 1968, 1972, and 1973) and was runner-up once. He also fostered the swings of Hollis Stacy, who also captured the Open title three times, as well as Bert Yancey and Ralph Johnson from the PGA Tour.

Flick was also active in the PGA of America, staging seminars, teaching workshops, and volunteering to direct programs for the National Golf Foundation. He was named PGA Teacher of the Year in 1988 and has accrued many other industry honors, awards, and accolades.

In 1974, fellow teacher Bob Toski invited Flick to become part of a new golf school program he was developing for *Golf Digest* magazine. Believing that golf instruction at that time was in dire straits, Toski recruited a number of top teachers to join him in establishing a nationwide program of schools under the aegis of the magazine. "Bob and I became heavily involved in the project, and we ended up doing those schools pretty much full time," Flick says. "I think we set the benchmark for golf schools at that time."

Indeed, the Golf Digest Golf Schools have been one of the most successful business operations over the last twenty years. In addition to teaching a full slate of courses for the schools, Flick contributed often to the magazine's instructional features and continued his work with professional golfers.

In 1990 he added an important new client. Jack Nicklaus traveled that year to Phoenix, Arizona, where Flick spent his winters, to compete in the inaugural The Tradition tournament, held on a course Nicklaus had designed at Desert Mountain in Scottsdale. "He hadn't been playing very well," Flick recalls. "Of course, I had known Jack since he was a kid back in Ohio, and I would see him from time to time and exchange pleasantries with him. At Desert Mountain that year, I spent some time working with him before the tournament, and he went out and played well and won it. Then he went to Augusta the next week and played well there, too."

As a result of those sessions, a seed of an idea was planted. Realizing that they shared a similar teaching philosophy, Nicklaus eventually proposed that Flick put together a special program. The result was the Nicklaus-Flick Golf Schools. Jim Flick (working as an employee of Golden Bear, Inc.) does the teaching; Jack Nicklaus provides his name and backing but does no teaching himself. It is a testament to Flick's experience and expertise that Nicklaus entrusts him to teach under the Bear's own name. Flick oversees the program's schools in Florida and in his home in the Arizona desert. In the summer, Flick and the schools move north to Michigan, where they operate at the Boyne Highlands Resort and other locations.

Flick has obviously spent many years in the trenches teaching and learning from all levels of players: from the struggling novice to some of the greatest players of our age. From this experience he's sharpened his philosophy.

"I began to notice, after talking with the Watsons and Players and Palmers and Nicklaus and even back to Sam Snead, that there is a great difference between how a player approaches playing the game and the way many teachers teach the game," Flick reflects. "Teachers have a tendency to break the swing down into individual pieces. Players talk about the game in terms of feel, rhythm, and execution. There's a huge difference."

Flick has come to believe that players, especially the good ones, don't want their swings broken down into so many little pieces and put back together. Players prefer a simple, holistic solution to the game, not a fragmented approach. Flick freely admits that early in his career he was in the forefront of the tear-a-swing-apart-and-put-it-back-together school. But his thinking and his teaching have evolved. "I've come to understand how so many approach the game so mechanically, so swing-focused," he says. "Then, once they get on the golf course, particularly in the 'part shots'—chipping and pitching and recovery shots that make up sixty percent of one's score—they don't know how to do it. They don't know how much swing to use because they're too busy turning the shoulders and driving the legs. They have no feeling for the rhythm or the speed."

Fundamental to Jim Flick's thoughts on the swing is that the motion of the arms turns the shoulders, rather than the turning of the shoulders making the arms move. Why is this so critical? Because swinging the arms first helps a player develop a sense of the golf club and begins the rhythm of the swing. "That's how players play," he says, "By using the golf club."

Flick believes that one should teach the short game, the part shots, first, before delving into the full swing. He understands that young players have a need to learn to hit the ball hard, but he has come to believe that teaching a player how to score with the short game, and thus gain some immediate and rewarding success on the golf course, is of paramount importance.

When it comes to the full swing, Flick first stresses an elementary question: what type, or shape, of ball flight does the student want? "It scares me that even good players go to see teachers who never ask what kind of ball flight they want. It's amazing!" he says. "If you want to fade the ball, the aim must be in one place, the grip and the pressure are such a way, and the swing must have a certain shape. If you want to draw the ball, there's a whole different set of factors that come in."

Flick believes in teaching a golf swing, not a golf hit. "Teach people to swing, and they can learn to hit," he insists. From the swing comes the sense of feel for the club and the rhythm of its movement that he believes is so important for good players to understand. He adds that there is no such thing as the perfect swing. Each golfer has physical and even mental characteristics that make each swing different.

Take a look, Flick says, at the top five golfers in history: Nicklaus, Hogan, Snead, Byron Nelson, and Bobby Jones. "Now it's funny," he says, "but none of them have very good-looking swings! And all of them have very different swings."

Nicklaus grew up in Ohio playing at the Scioto Country Club, where he needed a very high, soft ball flight to come down on the course's hard and smallish greens. On the other side of the coin, Ben Hogan grew up in Texas, on a wide-open, windy plain. He needed a low ball with a trajectory to bore through the wind, an approach quite different from Nicklaus's. Nelson needed a swing that helped him control the steel shafts that were still new in his era, so he had an inside dropping motion to keep his club from going outside. Bobby Jones played with hickory shafts early in his career, so he adopted a soft, syrupy swing to fit his equipment.

"Now, can you say any one of these swings was wrong?" Flick asks rhetorically. "Hell no! Take a look at the next level of the best golfers in history. There'll be disagreement in who ranks where, but you've got Palmer, Player, Casper, Trevino, Watson, Floyd, Sarazen, Hagen, Faldo, Price, Peter Thompson, Bobby Locke, Henry Cotten—and no two of those great players have swings that are alike. Now there may be certain ingredients that make the swing easier to repeat, but when we try to make everyone swing the same and do the same thing, I think we're going the wrong way."

Flick distinguishes two types of swings: a swing that uses the hands and wrists, and a swing of the arms that moves the hands, the wrists, and the club. The two swings share an emphasis on weight of the clubhead and its centrifugal force. He is concerned that today's modern equipment, which is getting lighter and lighter, is in danger of eliminating the weight of the clubhead and its important feel. "There's no question you can swing a light club faster, but does it have the same feel?" he asks. "Does it get the same characteristics that heavier clubs get? I'm not so sure I want to throw away decades of pure play because machinery tests equipment that swings faster and is lighter if it destroys the feel factor. After all, there aren't any damn machines leading the money list!"

Flick remembers one student who had a five handicap, but who won the club championship. This golfer didn't play a lot and had an unusual swing, but he was a fierce competitor in the short game. After he won the club tournament, he told Flick, "Now that I know I can win, I want to change my swing and make it simpler." Flick agreed to do it. "So we tore his natural swing up and he never could play as well ever again," he says. "Part of it was that he just didn't have the time a guy needs to make a major swing change and practice it. But just making a swing simpler doesn't help a guy; it has to be able to repeat. If a guy has a swing that repeats, he knows what

kind of ball flight he's going to get, he knows his circumstances, and he's comfortable with it; changing his swing
to look better isn't the answer."

That's why the mission of Flick's golf schools is to
help students play better golf, not swing better. Flick
remembers asking Nicklaus before the formation of their
school which of the younger Tour players had a swing he
admired. Jack thought a while and finally admitted, "Not
too many." Pressed, he said many of the younger players'
emphasis on swing mechanics failed to take into account
other important elements of the game. "He gave me a
quote which I think is the most articulate thing I've ever
heard about the game," Flick says. "He said 'Golf is a
game of emotion and adjustment.'"

Emotion and adjustment. Knowing your own mind
and body well enough to play the percentage shot at the
time it's called for. Being able to make the adjustments
necessary to make the shots. Nicklaus and Flick believe
that is the essence of championship golf.

That's why Flick teaches students how to use the
instrument of golf: the club. The body doesn't move to
move the club, the use of the club makes the body move.
In this, Flick echoes teachers of earlier decades, such as
Ernest Jones and his "swing the clubhead" methods.

Do you move your body when you putt, pivoting?
Of course not. You don't, Flick maintains, because the distance to the target does not require major motion. The
swinging of the putter to that target does not require one
to make a pivot or take a divot. On a chip shot, the body

does move slightly because the swing to that distance shot requires it. On a pitch shot, the distance is longer, and the pivot of the body is greater. And so on. The use of the club is what determines how much body motion is required.

"That's why I try to get people to use the instrument to make the ball go to the target," he says. "The body must find itself moving to the speed of the club. That's why you see guys with great rhythm, their bodies are moving in time to the club. Those who don't have good rhythm are trying to make the club move in time with their bodies. The club has no awareness, so it can't adjust."

In the Nicklaus-Flick schools, Jim Flick and his instructors do teach mechanics, but not at the expense of a golfer's feel. Flick calls it bridging the gap between the training ground and the play ground. "Once you're on the golf course, the conscious mind will try to destroy the subconscious and all the golf habits you've built up. It's not unlike when a football team calls a time out to freeze the opponent's field goal kicker before a crucial play. In most other games, one is reacting and the conscious mind has no time to get involved. In golf, the mind becomes either an asset or a liability in the way it's used. You've got to have an approach that allows you to learn the game in a manner that helps you play golf. Play golf means to have fun. Most people are working on the course."

Flick has gleaned a great deal from his interaction with Jack Nicklaus. For instance, he says, Nicklaus taught him that golf is not a position game, it's a motion game. "You need to learn position, but you can't let the position destroy the motion."

During his years of teaching and observing other instructors, Flick has noted a wide array of different teaching approaches. Harvey Penick, he says, taught by the guide and discovery method. He'd suggest a student try something and let that student find out for himself the beneficial results. That would help the student gain confidence in himself when it came time on the course for the emotion and adjustment Nicklaus talked about.

Many have long felt that Jack Nicklaus' own golf instructional books and videos are broad and overgeneralized. Jim Flick knows why. "I watched Jack work with his longtime teacher Jack Grout at Frenchman's Creek," he says. "Mr. Grout was very broad and general in how he taught the game." Yet another instructor working at the same club, Gardner Dickenson, is very specific in his instruction, the antithesis of Grout.

From those experiences, Flick has learned to pay attention to the student, find out what his or her particular needs are, and tailor an instructional program to fit. "It took me a long time to learn that," he admits. "I did a lot of studying and reading. I've read just about every book that's been written on the golf swing. And I began to realize that all these writers felt like they had the perfect golf swing for everybody. Well, there ain't no such thing!"

One of Flick's current professional clients is Ed Humenik. Flick immediately realized that because of

Humenik's build—he's short and stocky with short arms and a handsy swing—he wasn't able to bring his arms back to a position that other golfers easily attain. Taking into account the handsy nature of his swing, Flick helped him to refine rather than fix it. Two others Flick has worked with are Phil Blackmar and John Adams, both of whom are very tall. "I gotta teach them based on their properties as individuals," he says. "If I tried to teach only one swing for everybody, I'd end up helping only a few and hurting a few."

Flick also works closely with Tom Lehman, one of the bright new stars on the PGA Tour. "He recently gave me what I thought was the highest compliment. He said, 'We're now on our fourth year of working together, and we're still working on the same things we started in our first lesson.' That told me that we're not fooling around with differing philosophies, we're just looking for more knowledge. I've tried to give him the tools to simplify his swing so he can use his golf club. And make no mistake, he is a player not a swing freak. He played extremely well and was contending in the U.S. Open in 1995 at Shinnecock, and he admitted afterwards that he only had his B game that week. Now that's a player, someone who can find a way to make it happen even with only his B game."

Working with professional golfers is one thing. But working with the variety of handicaps of the golfers at the Nicklaus-Flick school sessions is another. Flick understands these golfers as well as anybody, however. He teaches, by his own estimate, 300 days per year, conducting as many as forty-five schools. That's given him a vast reservoir of experience to call on.

"In a school setting, you've got to learn how to get your message across quickly, succinctly, and simply," he says. "Some students want to know all the whys and wherefores, while others just want [you to give them] the information and then get the hell out of their way! Part of the art of teaching is watching and understanding people and looking for clues on how to get inside their minds, and you've got to do that differently with every person you teach."

Flick's primary goal is to help a student develop the feel involved in imparting the right message to the ball to direct it to the target area. He admits that this sounds too simplistic, but he believes it is the most fundamental goal of golf instruction. "We need to retreat to that, to the simplest level," he says. "You can't be complex and play well."

Interestingly, Flick likes to begin his school sessions by watching his students play. He wants to see how they aim, what their characteristics are, and what philosophies govern their play. He can tell a lot about a golfer by watching his demeanor, how and why he makes his club selections, and how he reacts to both good and bad shots. He places balls sixty yards from the green and observes who can pitch it onto the putting surface. His unscientific survey over the years indicates that fewer than a third of golfers can get a ball on the green from that distance.

"And if that's all—thirty-three percent—who can make that kind of shot, which represents the scoring part of the game, what does that say about the kind of golf instruction being taught in our country today?" He leaves the question unanswered, but it's clear his opinion is "not much."

In a session with a pro client, Flick will take him out to the hardest handicap hole on the course and watch what he does. On the range, he's learned, a professional golfer will hit balls until he eventually finds a workable solution to a swing problem. But on the golf course, a hard hole opens a little window into that golfer's soul that reveals much to Flick about his particular style.

"In a lot of schools, teachers will never see a student hit a ball other than on a practice range," Flick says. "That will not happen in my school. When you see a guy's decision-making process, his club selection philosophy, and how he handles trouble shots, you can help him become a better player."

To do that, he has recruited a top-level faculty of full-time teaching professionals who agree with his philosophy of teaching. One of his first hires for the Nicklaus-Flick program was Charley Epps. Flick admired Epps's holistic understanding of the game—both as a player and as a teacher. "I did not want to go down the road of the *Golf Digest* program, which just teaches how to swing the club," he said. "I wanted to teach how to play, and Charlie has helped me understand that better." Some of his other faculty members include Stan Thirsk, who has worked for years with Tom Watson; Dean Reinmuth, who works with Phil Mickelson; Mark Wood, whose pro clients include Dudley Hart and Joey Rasset; Mark Hall; and Ed Martin.

In his address to the PGA Teaching Summit on "How To Be A Master Teacher," Flick listed some teachers and instructors who he considered to be masters. He listed Ernest Jones, along with Tommy Armour, Harvey Penick, Bob Toski (who he called the best teacher the game's ever had), Seymour Dunn, and Manuel de la Torre.

And Jim Flick? "My goal in life is to see how good I can get and see if I can get there," he declares. "I do know this: I think everything moves in cycles, and I think the game is moving away from mechanics and back to teaching feel again. I hope so. I think that's the way the game needs to be taught."

Jim Flick

Practice Tee

Good posture is essential for efficient leg action. Here's a simple method to ensure good swing posture.

Hold a club across your hips, and with your knees locked, bend forward as if taking a bow. Let your posterior move back to counterbalance your upper body's forward tilt.

Slightly flex your knees three to four inches while keeping your weight over the balls of your feet.

Finally, grip the club with your arms hanging straight down from your shoulders.

This posture minimizes tension in your legs and gives the club and arms plenty of room to swing under your torso.

Chapter Six

RICK SMITH

THE PERIPATETIC ENTREPRENEUR

It just happened that on the day I played the Rick Smith course at Michigan's Treetops Resort, I was paired with a couple from Toledo, Ohio, who remembered when Smith was a young assistant golf pro at the Toledo Country Club earlier in his career.

"Oh, I remember Rick," said the wife, "All the women at the club wanted to take lessons with him. He was so cute!"

Some might say it's this sex appeal that has thrust Smith into the teaching spotlight. But most would attribute his burgeoning fame and reputation to his ceaseless energy and fertile mind. (Of course the good looks don't hurt.) Rick is a golf-school operator, swing consultant to a growing list of PGA Tour stars, golf course architect, TV star, and author; it's amazing that he has time to eat and sleep. But Smith enjoys his hectic schedule—"It keeps me fresh."

Born in Coldwater, Michigan, Rick Smith moved
with his family to Upper St. Clair, a suburb of Pittsburgh,
when he was six years old. He played many sports as a
kid, but was drawn into golf by the successes of his older
brother; Rick caddied for his brother when he won the
club championship at the tender age of sixteen.

Smith himself was soon capturing trophies as a
junior. He garnered numerous local titles and was
ranked among the top five juniors in the country. As the
Pennsylvania high school state champion, Smith was
courted with several college scholarships. Despite generous offers from Wake Forest, Florida State, and
Florida, he surprisingly accepted an offer from East
Tennessee State. "I liked the coach, Hal Morrison, the
school was only a six-hour drive from Pittsburgh, and
they were ranked fourth in the country at the time,"
Smith explains.

The young freshman jumped onto the first team,
playing in the number two position. East Tennessee,
although small, competed against a number of big-name
schools in collegiate tournaments. But the campus in
Johnson City, high in the Appalachians, does not have
year-round golfing weather, as Smith soon discovered, and
he wanted to work on his golf game, if not his tan, all
year. So he transferred to Brevard Junior College in Florida
and helped that team win the NCAA title.

After earning his associate degree at twenty, Rick
Smith turned professional and took a job as assistant pro
with Don Cotten at the Toledo Country Club, where he set

female hearts aflutter. "Don allowed me to teach, and I really got into it," Smith says. "But I still wanted to play and had my heart set on making it to the Tour one day." The young pro appeared in local tournaments, played various courses in an effort to break their scoring records, and once participated in a fundraising marathon for charity—he played 523 holes in one day.

Earning his Class A PGA of America credentials, Smith moved on to the Scioto Country Club in Columbus, the fabled club at which Jack Nicklaus cut his teeth. "I learned a lot about the traditions of the game there," Smith says. "Everyone at Scioto is proud of the game and the role that club has played in its development since the early 1900s." Smith worked at Scioto under head pro Walker Inman from 1982 until 1984, teaching and learning the business of running a golf shop.

And he still kept his hand in playing. Smith qualified for the U.S. Open at Oakmont in 1983 and played in the PGA Assistant Pro's Championship. He also spent a year at the River Oaks Club in Houston, working for Dick Harmon and getting to know his brothers and father.

In 1985 Harry Melling, owner and developer of Treetops outside Gaylord, Michigan, persuaded the young pro to return to his home state to help further develop the growing resort. At the time Smith arrived in 1986, Treetops had just one golf course, designed by Robert Trent Jones. Today it has a Tom Fazio course as well as two Rick Smith designs (a championship course and a nine-hole par-three course) and is awaiting the grand opening of a third.

His playing career took a detour, however, soon after he accepted the job at Treetops. He slipped on some steps at the resort, breaking his knee and spraining his shoulder. Although fully recovered and feeling competitive again, his work as a teacher and lately as a golf course architect has superseded his desire to win golf tournaments.

From the beginning, Rick Smith had been a student of the golf swing, even as a youngster. He had been taught as a junior by Jim Ferree and always watched the great golfers in hopes of picking up swing tips. "I tried to study the swings of everyone to figure out what was best for me," he says. "I watched Nicklaus, Trevino, and Watson because I wanted to find out which swing would work for me. I mimicked all of them."

His swing ended up a combination of everyone's: Nicklaus, Watson, Crenshaw, Hogan, and even Johnny Miller thrown in for good measure. Smith was always visually oriented; he would pour over swing photos and then try to put those pictures into dynamic action. "I learned a lot from watching and studying the swing," he says. "It helped me both as a player and as a teacher." In fact, he often found himself giving tips to his teammates in high school and college. "I could see faults and tried to fix them with my buddies even back then," he admits. "Sometimes I'd ask myself, 'What are you doing? You should be working on your own game!'"

His study of swings has given him a keen eye that quickly discerns a golfer's characteristics and where corrections are needed. Smith calls them the variables of a swing. Understanding a player's game as a whole is as important as understanding his swing. Seeing the variables at work in the bigger picture allows him to see that if one part is out of kilter it will show up in another part of the swing. "When I work with my pro clients, I understand how they should be and how they were when they were playing well," he says. "And I understand the variables when they go in the wrong direction. Like if Zinger [Paul Azinger] changes his grip but everything else in his swing stays the same, I can tell him that when you make one adjustment usually another's got to go. They go hand in hand."

Smith says he is not a method teacher, per se, but does believe in selected fundamentals. For him, the most important of these may be body motion, something he stresses over and over both with his golf school students and his professional clients. "Body motion is critical," he asserts. "It's important to understand it. We do a lot of mirror work to get golfers in a position that shows they aren't tilted in the upper body while their hips slide to the right. That's a huge problem with many players."

Smith notes that many players, especially the more talented ones, get too steep on their backswings, forcing them to slide with their bodies. This in turn works the club underneath the plane coming down, resulting in either a flip hook or an off-center hit.

He also teaches feel, a sense of the clubhead moving back and through. He emphasizes the role of feel in monitoring pace and rhythm. Smith believes that golfers must have an awareness of where their club is during the swing, which is his definition of feel. He says, "You look at some of the odd golf swings and try to figure out why they work. The only explanation is that they're very aware of their wrong move, which helps create a right move. Of course, I don't teach that, but I understand it and respect it."

As a player himself, Smith knows that the fewer compensations, the easier it is to play the game. As a teacher, when he suggests an adjustment, he understands what makes the adjustment work.

Smith's sharp eye and deep study of the golf swing has paid off in his work with professional clients. Although he followed the path of a club professional and taught clinics, ladies, and juniors along the way, he has also been lucky enough to hook up with touring pros who have gone on to glory and brought other impressive names into the Smith fold.

His first client was Rocco Mediate, whom he met when Rocco was on the golf team at Florida Southern College and Smith was working winters at a club in Lakeland, Florida. Mediate's first year on the Tour was tough. He won only $20,670, finished 174th on the money list, and lost his card. "After that first year he came to me and said, 'I can't play out there; I'm not going to last. What can I do?' We made some huge changes in his swing."

Following that winter of work, Rocco re-earned his Tour card by finishing second in the qualifying tourna-

ment—and he never looked back. After four seasons of
steady improvement on the Tour, Rocco broke through
with a 1991 win at the Doral Ryder tournament in Miami.
"It was exciting to watch his first win at Doral," Smith
remembers. "He was my first student to win. I thought of
all the hard work he put in when he beat Curtis Strange in
a playoff, and—suddenly bang! He's the leading money
winner on Tour!"

His success with Rocco prompted another Florida
Southern alumnus to seek Smith's aid. "I first met Lee
Janzen when he was just a kid from Lakeland," he recalls.
"He'd come pick up balls at the practice range in exchange
for golf lessons. I tried to help him with his fundamentals,
tried to make sure he wasn't going in the wrong direction."

Smith noticed that Janzen had that intangible quality that defines great players. "He was persistent, stubborn,
and a hard-working kid," Smith says. "Those are good
signs in a kid. I could see him becoming a competitor
when he was in high school. He hated to embarrass himself; he always wanted to play well. And he worked hard.
I can see him with that big head of curly hair, standing
around watching, always watching, and copying things.
Back then, we all thought I was going to be the player, so
he'd watch me hit balls by the hour."

Smith continued to foster Janzen's game through
college and on to the PGA Tour, which he joined in 1990.
His first win came at the 1992 Northern Telecon Open in
Tucson. And in 1993, after a win at the Phoenix Open,
Janzen topped the Tour's money list going into the U.S.

Open, and going out, after he claimed the national title at Baltusrol.

Suddenly, Rick Smith, swing guru, was in demand as never before. Life was rosy and getting even rosier.

While working at Treetops with Chris Rule, a young collegiate golfer from Ohio State, he met one of Chris's teammates and buddies, Gary Nicklaus, son of the Golden Bear. During a Florida swing when Smith had been grooming Janzen, Rule set up an appointment and told Smith he was bringing Gary with him. After a few days on the course together, Gary invited Smith to "come over to the house and we'll go the range."

When Rick arrived at the West Palm Beach Nicklaus compound, father Jack answered the front door. "I think he wanted to know more about me," Smith laughs about that first meeting with the golfing legend. The Nicklauses and Smith went out to the practice range, where Jack asked if Smith would watch him hit balls.

"I said, 'Sure. Let's do it!'" Smith recalls. "I'd studied Jack's swing for years, and I knew what made it work. I saw that his body had changed a lot. I knew he had been working out with weights for some time, and he was real tight. I suggested he try swinging a heavy club, but he had hurt his arm. Even though Jack works out daily, he's had a lot of nagging injuries."

Nicklaus warmed to Smith's suggestions, and the two have worked occasionally together ever since. Smith's efforts to get Jack's swing looser and more flexible never cease. "That's been the biggest challenge, flexibility," he says. "It shows in his driving. He used to have this big arc, get really deep into the swing, back behind the ball beautifully, then hit it from the inside perfectly, usually with that big high fade." Smith has also helped Nicklaus draw the ball on occasion. "He was picking the club up, crossing the line, working it back under the plane, and flip-hooking it," he says. "I told him, that's not the way you need to draw the ball. Let's fix the backswing, and then you can draw it or fade it."

Smith insists that working on the swing of the greatest golfer of all time never intimidated him. "You just have to trust your eyes," he states matter-of-factly. "There are certain things a player wouldn't see until you can show him on video. Jack would take a look at himself and say, 'If I knew I was doing that, I would have changed it!'"

Smith still advises Gary Nicklaus, too, and has enjoyed his association with the family. He understands that Jack still goes to others for occasional brush-ups—Jim Flick and others—but, Smith says, "He still wants my eyes on him from time to time, and that's an honor."

It's also a good calling card. Smith has worked with Billy Andrade for several years, since Billy's teacher, Davis Love Jr., died in a plane crash. He's also trained his talented eyes on Curtis Strange, Tom Kite, Billy Glasson, and others. "It's a thrill when they say, 'Can I borrow your eyes for a while?'" he says. "When they do well, you just feel great inside. When they do poorly, you feel terrible and partly responsible."

Smith likes to consider his clients his friends, too. "I want them to do well, and I'm always calling them, just to see how they are, what's up in their lives," he says. "Most of the guys I work with are friends of mine, and I like to keep it that way."

He is frankly uncomfortable with establishing a business relationship with these friends. One gets the sense that he doesn't like to discuss fees for his teaching expertise. "My financial situation is OK with my design business and running the resort and my other teaching, so I'm not out to solicit a lot of business from the Tour," he says. "When my pros play well, the last thing I want is some of their money. Occasionally they'll fire me something because of the time and effort I spend, but I try to just throw it back. Jack tried to do that, and I said I don't want it. He wanted to at least reimburse me for travel and hotels, but I don't like to do that. My whole feeling is just having a love for the game and sharing my expertise with people."

He shares that expertise with a great many people at the sessions of the Rick Smith Golf Academy held at Treetops every summer, most of which are usually fully booked with long waiting lists. He is as enthusiastic about teaching ordinary golfers as he is spending a few hours with a Nicklaus or a Janzen. "I love beginners," he exclaims. "I love to get them all excited and pumped up about their golf game. For some of these guys, who've spent a lifetime battling a big slice, when you can show them how to hit a little draw, or even a block, or show them how to turn a big slice into a little slice, well, they start jumping up and down!"

Smith aims to keep his schools to a maximum of four students per session, and with his school director Henry Young and a few assistant teachers, he can offer a student to teacher ratio of 2:1. Yes, he uses the video, the computer programs, the swing aids, and the teaching equipment, but for the most part he's a hands-on teacher.

"I get them into exaggerated modes of change and show them it's okay," he says. "The mind hates to make changes. With pros, you're dealing with fractions and variables that are very sensitive at their level. If they're off, they're way off. But with amateur players, you have to encourage them to change something, and then when they do it, you have to praise them up and down. And they say, 'But I still missed it!'."

Smith understands that psychology plays a major part in teaching golf. Pros have a higher risk involved in making swing changes, but amateur players are faced with their pride, peer pressure, and other imposing elements. Humiliation and its avoidance is a prominent issue of modern golf. "Arnold Palmer once said, 'Golf seems so simple, but it's endlessly complicated,' And he's right," Smith says. "You have to try and get people to realize that."

These days when he's not teaching, which is rarely, Rick Smith wears the hard hat of a golf course architect. It was an unplanned career move. When he arrived at Treetops in 1986, the resort had just one golf course. But owner Harry Melling had hired Tom Fazio to build a second, and as golf director, Smith was involved in the design and construction. He studied these processes with the same zeal as he had studied the elements of the golf swing.

After a visit to Augusta National and the Masters one year, Smith returned to Michigan eager to build a par-three course like the one at Augusta. Watching the fun of the annual par-three tournament held the Wednesday afternoon of Masters week, he realized the resort setting was ideally suited for a similar facility. Harry Melling gave Smith the green light, so he designed and built the par-three course. Its entertaining layout is often used as a warm-up before a round on the "big course" and has become the site of many a wager. Smith also designed an elaborate practice range for the Academy and a severely undulating putting course for the Treetops North complex that adjoins the Fazio course.

The next year, Melling gave him a compass and a 350-acre plot saying, "Go build a golf course."

"It seems like my whole life has worked in similar fashion, whether it's teaching or design," Smith says. "In teaching, I spent all that time studying golf swings. In design, I spent a lot of time with Robert Trent Jones and Tom Fazio, learning all that I could about that craft. In fact, I realized that I had always paid close attention to golf courses, clubhouses, and pro shops with an idea of what I liked and what worked and what didn't."

Smith devoted countless hours to the design of his first full eighteen-hole course. "I didn't want to make any mistakes," he said. "I wanted to build something that fits the land and brings out the views." The Rick Smith Signature course at Treetops is a beautifully playable design that starts atop a hillside and meanders down a broad valley below. Because the course is designed mainly for resort guests, the fairways are wide and forgiving, but Smith built expansive greens and rigged them with abundant movement and undulation. He framed the bunkers with long-growing native fescues that create a wild look while clearly defining the limits of the hazards. And he left most approaches open, bringing the bump and run shot back into the game.

"When you're teaching someone, you can see what goes in the air and what doesn't," he says. "But in design, you can't just create one shot to make it a great hole. You have to have a variety of angles and different things that can challenge and reward a player and not severely penalize him."

Rick Smith's first golf course was so well received by the public that Harry Melling had no qualms about giving him another commission. "Harry's been great," Smith says. "I'll go to him with an idea and say, 'What do you think?' and he'll say, 'Let's do it!'" The latest project is one that's close to Smith's heart: a golf course designed to be walked. No carts will be allowed on the new course when it opens in 1996, and Smith will oversee the development of a caddie program for the resort. "It's been great, and

the feedback I've gotten from people has been wonderful," he says. "There are some skeptics, of course, but
most people think bringing walking back into the game is
good for golf, a good idea."

Smith is also excited about another project that's
under construction. He's building a golf course for a private club in Holland, Michigan, near Grand Rapids. "It's
one of those rare birds in golf," he says. "A club for players. Fifteen multimillionaires put down $10 million and
said, 'Go build a great golf course.' It's a beautiful site with
rivers and streams. I think it's going to be a beautiful
thing."

Smith plans to expand his golf course design business, bringing his professional clients along as guest con-
sultants. His design business now has a staff of three. "I'll
go from the practice range, put on my boots and hard hat,
and switch gears," he says. "It keeps me fresh and enthusiastic, although you have to learn how to switch the dials. I
don't want to get burned out in just one area, so this way,
I can switch back and forth and still always be fresh."

And that's not all for the peripatetic Smith. He has
hosted a popular instructional golf show in Canada for the
last few years, which was recently picked up by ESPN and
sponsored by Ford Electronics. This is in addition to his
Practice Range instructional video, which has been a hot
seller. Also in the works: a software program that contains
all the different golf swings and variations to help average
players understand their own swings—and how to
improve them.

And finally, working with a cousin, who is a major outlet mall developer, Smith wants to start a chain of Rick Smith Practice Centers that will feature indoor and outdoor hitting areas, nine-hole par-three courses, and practice holes along with fully stocked pro shops selling equipment and clothing to golfers. "If it works, we hope to have fifteen centers up and running in the next five years," he predicts. "And all of them will have quality instruction."

For Smith, it all comes back to the lesson tee. "I love teaching and I always will," he says. "My focus and love is always there. No matter what else I'm doing, I'm teaching three days a week at least."

Rick Smith

Practice Tee

Many amateurs swing past parallel, causing their arms to collapse and the swing arc to narrow dramatically. A common result of this out-of-control backswing is a quick uncocking (casting) of the hands and wrists that creates a poor impact position, i.e. usually an open clubface position, but sometimes, a closed clubface position.

To counter the cast, concentrate on setting the right arm in an "L" at the top of the swing. The forearm (wrist to elbow) should be virtually vertical; the upper arm (elbow to shoulder) should be parallel to the ground. Ideally, the clubshaft will be parallel to the ground, too.

Attaining and holding the "L" position promotes the proper unhinging of the right arm and wrist on the downswing, and, with that, a square impact position.

—originally published in *GOLF* magazine

Chapter Seven

CHUCK HOGAN

A DIFFERENT DRUMMER

Millions upon millions of golfers struggle almost daily to master the game of golf. They have bookshelves crammed with how-to golf manuals, they study the television set every weekend searching for hints from the weekend warriors of the Tour, and they pour over the magazines that arrive each month looking for the tip du jour that will unlock the elusive secrets of the perfect swing. But it doesn't seem to work. Week after week, month after month, year after year, this legion of frustrated golfers struggles to hit drives in fairways, approach shots on greens, and putts into holes. Sometimes they play well for a hole or two, but then that indescribable "it" goes away again, and balls squirt sideways, refuse to budge from bunkers, or ricochet off every tree in sight. The frustration meter explodes into the red zone.

Then along comes Chuck Hogan to remind them to relax, don't worry, golf's a pretty easy game, and it's all in your head anyway. Hogan likes to wear a sweatshirt to his golf schools that reads on the front, "Don't Sweat the Small Stuff." When he turns around, his students see: "It's All Small Stuff."

Hogan approaches the game from an unusual perspective. Most golfers have been conditioned to believe that golf is hard, almost impossible. The only way to improve at it is to practice this and practice that by the hour and move this body part here and that body part there. Even then, the secrets of the sport are murky and inaccessible.

By far, the majority of golfers never get past the mechanical rudiments of the sport because they have been taught, by whomever first showed them how to grip a club or by the television commentators or the magazine editors, that golf is about mastering the mechanics.

Chuck Hogan begs to differ. Hogan, the premiere teacher of the mental game of golf, has spent most of his career inveighing against those who preach mechanics, or at least mechanics as life itself. For Hogan firmly believes that swing mechanics are only a small factor in the equation for those who want to soar like the eagles on the golf course.

That kind of thinking is extemely hard for most golfers to swallow. But for those who get it, Hogan's ideas reveal an entirely different perspective on the game of golf, if not on life itself.

BUTCH HARMON

Courtesy PGA *Magazine*

DICK HARMON

Courtesy PGA *Magazine*

JIM MCLEAN   Courtesy Jim McLean Golf Schools

DAVID PELZ

RICK SMITH

©Dave Richards

©Dave Richards

JIM FLICK

CHUCK HOGAN

SHELBY FUTCH

SHELBY FUTCH

PEGGY KIRK BELL

©Dave Richards

JIM BALLARD

©Lafayette

DAVID LEADBETTER

©Michael Haddad

Chuck Hogan did not set out to become the chief iconoclast of golf, toppling the golf-is-a-mechanical-game temple. It just worked out that way.

Born in California, Hogan was raised in Redmond, Oregon, a backwater logging town where golf was a rare recreational pursuit. But his father played, and he had Chuck out on the course at age nine, using his mother's right-handed clubs, even though he was left-handed like his father.

He developed proficiency at the sport and played in enough junior tournaments to gain statewide attention and a scholarship from the University of Oregon. There, he picked up range balls for the coach of the team, Gary Wiren. The irony of a young Chuck Hogan playing for Wiren is delicious; Dr. Wiren, now a master PGA professional, is a high priest in the mechanics school of golf.

As might be expected, the young Hogan paid little attention to his coach. But as he admits now, it was mostly because as an eighteen-year-old going away to school in the mid-1960s, he was more interested in drinking beer, chasing coeds, and generally raising hell than in learning anything about golf. In any case, Hogan did not last. He dropped out after only a year at Oregon. With the Vietnam war raging in Southeast Asia, Hogan was soon drafted into the army.

About a year later, he was scheduled for deployment to Vietnam when he was diagnosed with a cancerous growth on his brain. After a six-month treatment of radiation, Hogan was given a clean bill of health and discharged.

Older and wiser now in many ways, he went back to school, this time enrolling in the Western Oregon College of Education. He majored in education not because he wanted to be a teacher, he says, but because he knew he wanted to become a teaching professional in golf and needed to know how and why people learn things.

Upon graduation, he began to work his way up in his chosen profession. He became an assistant pro at an Oregon club, later moved to the Sun River golf resort near Mount Hood, and finally joined the staff of a driving range and teaching facility in Eugene. There he got his first taste of golf instruction while conducting beginners' golf weekends, two-day clinics for roughly ten new golfers. Hogan showed them the proper grip, stance, and alignment. They whacked mountains of range balls, with Hogan dispensing tips as he paced up and down the line. After a little bunker practice and some putting at the end of the second day, Hogan made his good-work, keep-it-up, practice-hard farewell speech.

A student at one of these weekends told Hogan, "Chuck, this has been fun, but you haven't taught us anything about how to play golf."

For Hogan, it was an epiphany. He realized in a blinding flash of inspiration that his student was entirely correct. He had been teaching nothing about playing golf, but only the basic rudiments of how to swing a golf club. And he suddenly realized that most golfers spend their entire lives trying to play a game called golf swing, not golf itself.

The student's question crystallized for Hogan what had been troubling him for some time. Newcomers to the game, as well as those seeking improvement, were immediately sucked into the industry-wide model that focuses on the golf swing. The books, the magazines, and all the other teachers were worshipping at that altar, and for what? A lifetime of misery, because the golf swing is something that can never be entirely mastered or even definitively measured. Indeed, the high gospel of the mechanics-based instructional school is that the golf swing is difficult to learn and virtually impossible to perfect. In this model, the only solution is to practice endlessly, beating ball after ball.

"I realized, in one of those seminal 'a-ha!' moments, that those existing models and attitudes were a lot of crap, designed only to keep students in a constant state of frustration," Hogan says. "And I decided to create a different model."

Hogan knew from his educational background that the brain is bicameral. The left side of the brain controls the functions of logic and linear thinking. It is here that one calculates one plus one is two, figures out why water always runs downhill, and understands how to change a flat tire. The left brain is the thinking side, the serious side, the responsible side.

The right hemisphere of the brain, on the other hand, is the seat of creativity and imagination. It is where the artist sees the shape and understands the color, where the musician hears the harmonies of the spheres and the writer consults his Muse. It is the side of love, of playfulness, of eating strawberries and cream, and skinny dipping in the moonlight.

Scientists know that although these two parts of the brain seem in constant conflict, we in fact appear capable of occupying the middle ground between the two hemispheres, drawing on both sides as we perform the basic functions of life. Hogan realized that most golfers are stuck in the linear and logical swing mechanics of the left brain but that golf is a game best played from the right side, the creative and imaginative side.

So he proposed a new model for teaching golf rooted in this understanding. Mechanics can be learned, like driving a car, tying one's shoes, or swinging a golf club on the proper plane. All are linear functions that we practice, internalize, and in the end don't need conscious thought to perform. But for golf to be played well, it must be played with the full force of the creative side of the right brain at work. Hogan likes to remark that if we all tried to drive automobiles around town with the same mechanics-based throught processes that we use on the golf course, the streets would be littered with wrecks. And operating an automobile, he reminds us, requires far more physical and coordinative skills than swinging a golf club.

Fortuitously, perhaps, at the time of Chuck Hogan's conversion, a little book had just been published entitled *Golf in the Kingdom*, by Michael Murphy, the cofounder of the Esalen Institute on California's Big Sur coast. The now-famous book relates the story of a young golfer who makes a pilgrimage to Scotland where he happens upon a strange, mystical golf professional. The seer tells him not to keep the left arm straight and head down, but to think of the clubface and ball as becoming one and that the score is not important.

The book and its somewhat cosmic, antiworldly atmosphere sounded a harmonic chord within Hogan. He picked up the phone and called Murphy in San Francisco. He was invited to the author's home, where he spent several hours discussing the book, golf, and his nascent teaching model. It was only years later that he learned Michael Murphy is something of a recluse who has even turned down Carlos Castenada's requests for a meeting.

Hogan began to read: Maxwell Mault's *Psycho-Cybernetics*; Shakti Gawain's *Creative Visualization*; Korn & Johnson's *Visualization: The Uses of Imagery in the Health Professions*. As he read and studied and continued to teach golf at his facility in Eugene, Hogan began to develop his strange new model for teaching golf.

Obviously, learning mechanics is important. Golfers need to know how to grip the club, how to stand in relation to the ball, and how to move the club to make the ball do what they want. But Hogan came to believe that at some point, thinking about mechanics must end. And that time is when the golfer steps up to the first tee. From that point, he or she must instead be engaged solely in playing the game.

One of the most frustrating and yet insightful things people must learn about Chuck Hogan is the way he uses language. He tells those who insist that they must first have schooling in golf's fundamentals to examine the word. "It breaks down into FUN-da-MENTALs," he observes, completely ignoring all the rules of etymology. But he gets his point across that golf should be mentally fun, not hard work.

Likewise, when he says people should play golf, he is using the verb *to play* in its original sense—to act in a childlike manner. For most people, to play golf means to seriously pursue a lower score. It's a grinding and arduous pursuit. For people like that, even his touring professional clients, Hogan asks a simple question: "If you're not having fun, why are you doing this?" For Hogan, the concept of play is to act childlike, in the sense of being creative and imaginative, fully engaged in the activity of the moment. Children in a sandbox do not worry about technique or mechanics. They lose themselves in the act of playing in the sand and have a great time.

Hogan's goal has always been to help students find a way to lose themselves, or at least their conscious minds, in the act of playing on the golf course. He defines this state as being in the zone. Anyone who's played the game for long has probably experienced, if only for one shot, the zone. It is where golf happens effortlessly. It is splitting the fairways, booming a drive, striking iron shots on the sweet spot, seeing the ball roll across the green and dive into the hole. When you are in the zone, you don't have to try to make great or perfect shots; they seem to happen of their own accord. Michael Murphy writes of a golfer playing an entire round in the zone, describing it as walking downhill for the entire eighteen holes. Touring professionals, especially those who have won an important tournament, have learned how to stay in the zone for the better part of four rounds.

But conventional wisdom holds that the zone is as ephemeral as a rainbow; it comes and goes seemingly at will. There may be reasons why a twenty-handicapper can suddenly make three pars in a row, but they simply can't be explained. It should just be enjoyed while it lasts.

Hogan, as usual, refuses to buy into conventional wisdom. He has studied the zone, and dedicated his career as a teacher to helping golfers find ways to consciously enter it. In fact, being able to golf in the zone should be the only and ultimate goal of every golfer, he believes.

"What the playing of golf is has to do with getting lost and absorbed into the target and its conditions as well as the entire environment of the course," Hogan wrote in one of his books. "It's about merging into the wind, the humidity, the lie of the ball, length of the shot, roll of the putt, feel of the turf, texture of the sand—the way you feel physically, mentally, emotionally, and spiritually. It's the relative position of your score, your opponent's score, the demands of the shot, and your relationship to the field of players, past, present, and future. Golf evokes harmony or disharmony with the choice of clubs, the feel of the club, and how it can be artfully employed to meet your pre-viewed execution of the shot and of the accumulation of shots. The best of golf is the losing of oneself by the sim-ple love for hitting this ball into that hole."

By the late 1970s, Chuck Hogan had progressed far enough in his reading and study to teach golf in a way that was a radical departure from the rest of the industry. He launched the Chuck Hogan Golf School in Oregon in 1979. Some years later, he changed the name of his com-pany to Sports Enhancement Associates, or S.E.A. Although his teaching methods have evolved somewhat over the years, his program has always been consistent.

Hogan has always begun his workshops by devel-oping a behavioral profile of his golfing students. His col-lege training taught him that students learn in different ways at different speeds, and he always wondered why some golf students could get it while others couldn't. Hogan found the standard DISC psychological testing system helpful in pinpointing an individual's propensities for learning and doing, which came in handy when it was time to teach that student the game. Some people learn by watching another and imitating the motion. Others learn by listening to an explanation, internalizing the idea, and then following the directions. Others learn a task through a combination of watching, listening, and performing.

The DISC system distinguishes golfers' learning modes and playing styles. Hogan believes that acknow-ledging a player's personal style is essential to effective teaching. For instance, consider the last round of the 1995 British Open at St. Andrews in Scotland. Long John Daly was marching down the last few holes with a small lead. Watching from the television booth as a color commentator was Jack Nicklaus.

Nicklaus was aghast that Daly continued to pull his driver out of the bag on tee after tee, telling the television audience that the smarter and more conservative play would be to hit a safe iron into the fairway.

Hogan knows that Daly is a D player: he is decisive, he is dominant, he is direct, and he plays damn fast! He doesn't see trouble, because all he can see from the tee is his target. He swings hard, except for when he swings harder. This type of direct play can be stunning when the golfer's game is on, but when it isn't, it can be dangerous! That's John Daly in spades. Seen in this light, there should have been no surprise that Daly kept hitting driver after driver at the British Open; playing safe and conservative is simply not his style.

But that is precisely the style of a typical S player, who is singular, sensible, and strategic. These players may be slow in making up their minds, but once they have assembled all the data about the tournament or the hole or the shot, they move in strict accordance with what they have decided to do. Jack Nicklaus, of course, is the most prominent S player in history.

Thus Nicklaus, filtering what he was watching through his own playing propensities, was surprised at Daly's choices. Daly, in the meantime, probably thought he was playing smart golf by going with his strengths. The point is, they were both right.

Once he had students pegged, Hogan adapted the theories of neurolinguistic programming to the teaching of golf. These theories of behavioral science hold that we operate in life through a combination of language-learning and sensory response. Boiled down, this means that we are all guided by our senses, and usually one of those five senses is more dominant than others. In golf, three of the five senses come into play: sight, touch, and hearing (taste and smell are usually only utilized at the 19th hole).

Hogan helps a student find which of his senses is dominant; again, a battery of psychological and behavioral tests help identify propensities. Once he knows which sense is dominant, Hogan demonstrates how to take advantage of it to improve his game.

To do that requires the use of imagery. For instance, a large number of golfers are visually dominant. Jack Nicklaus is a good example of a visual player, Hogan says. Nicklaus has often said that he never selects a club until he can see in his mind's eye, the ball flying through the air and landing at the target—the spot that Nicklaus wants to reach with his next shot. Once Nicklaus has this picture clearly in mind, making the actual shot is easy.

But other golfers cannot see anything when they try to visualize a shot. Instead, these golfers play by a sense of kinesthetic feel. When they are playing well, they get a warm, fuzzy feeling inside or in a certain part of their body. They may not be able to see a shot in advance like Nicklaus, but they can concentrate on feeling a "go signal" that gives them the internal confidence to make a shot.

A third group of golfers is auditory. These are the tempo players who swing to an internal rhythm all their own. Watch the old tapes of Bobby Jones, one of the greatest of all auditory players, and you will witness a graceful choreography as he approaches the ball, waggles, and swings. There is never a moment in a Jones swing in which something is not moving, yet it all coalesces into a perfect, rhythmic whole.

Auditory golfers must tune in to their internal sense of rhythm and tempo to play their best. Unlike visual golfers, who can tell you where their hands are at every point of the swing, or kinesthetic golfers, who can tell you how a golf swing feels, auditory golfers simply let the motion guide their swings.

Teaching golfers inward-looking, imagery-based techniques was radical stuff in the '70s and '80s, but Hogan found that many of his students thrived within this new model. Certainly, telling a golfer to imagine a Day-Glo pink green in the distance as the target and to imagine a line of bright green worms pointing the way to the hole is a far cry from telling a golf student to keep his head down, his left arm straight, and swing from the inside out.

Hogan moved S.E.A. to Sedona, Arizona, in the early 1980s. Sedona, of course, is well known as a New Age headquarters where a supposed harmonic convergence has attracted crystal gazers, Tarot readers, and other adherents of the strange and wonderful. But Hogan says he selected the location only because of a newspaper article that called it one of the ten best places in the country to raise children.

There, Hogan began producing his golf books and video tapes, which have always been among the best-selling instructional items in the industry. His first video, *Nice Shot!*, explained in simple terms Hogan's unusual concepts. His first book, *Five Days to Golfing Excellence*, went into more complex detail. Yet even today both video and book rank among the top-selling instructional materials available.

In the early 1980s a college professor from Boston sought Hogan out and showed him his experiments in using sound technology to create deeper levels of imagery. The use of the synthetic sounds was supposed to stimulate the brain to drop into deeper levels of consciousness, making the elusive zone more accessible. Hogan was intrigued by the method and began to incorporate the sound tapes in his schools as a way for golfers to explore self-imagery. For a guinea pig he called on fellow Oregonian and PGA Tour player Peter Jacobsen, who agreed to work with the tapes and with Hogan's system.

Within a few weeks of working with Hogan,
Jacobsen won the Colonial National Invitational at Fort
Worth (in 1984). After dominating the Greater Hartford
Open later that year, he began publicly lauding Hogan's
rather strange theories. Other touring pros began calling,
their interest picqued. Soon Hogan was priming Mike
Reid, D.A. Weibring, Johnny Miller, as well as several
LPGA golfers on his new theories.

One night at 4 a.m., Hogan's telephone rang. It was
Raymond Floyd, calling from Scotland and the British
Open. Floyd, intensely curious about Hogan's ideas,
wished to discuss them further on the practice range.
Hogan eventually helped Floyd discover a visual acuity
problem that had affected his putting. The problem cor-
rected, Floyd went on to win the 1986 U.S. Open.

Hogan has also instructed collegiate golfers. He has
consulted with the Arizona State University and UCLA
women's golf teams and conducts clinics and seminars for
both golfers and coaches at the collegiate and junior levels.

Hogan eventually abandoned the sound tapes; he
found that both professional and amateur clients reported
that after returning to normal, workaday worlds, they
abandoned the daily tape-meditation sessions. Nobody
else was working with anything remotely like Hogan's
tapes, and when medical science labeled the brain-wave
activity Hogan believed held the secret to the zone as
"altered states of consciousness," he knew the battle was

lost. He could hardly instruct Tour stars to do something they were told was similar to taking LSD.

Many of Hogan's experimental teachings over the years have suffered the same fate. Nevertheless, some of his innovations have taken hold. Told for years that he couldn't in good conscience completely ignore the teaching of golf mechanics, Hogan finally wrote a book on the subject for beginners, *Learning Golf*, which, of course, tells them how to get past mechanics as soon as possible. Believing that putting depends largely on proper eyesight and alignment, Hogan developed a video teaching aid called *Aim to Win*, which helps golfers identify their dominant eye and use it to sink more putts.

As Chuck Hogan continues to plumb the science of psychoneurology to better understand the human brain and its potential, he constantly seeks input from his professional clients.

As a result, he has discovered that top touring pros do indeed possess a secret weapon that amateur players almost uniformly lack: a sense of safety on the golf course. Whether through some acquired process, because of fortuitous upbringing, or just by luck, the top players of the world have learned to feel comfortable in what the rest of us would judge to be anxiety-producing, high-stress situations. Whether driving down the 18th fairway in a major tournament with a one-stroke lead or attempting to make a birdie to catch the leader, a top-notch golfer won't buckle under pressure.

To most of us, who struggle to make a three-footer to clinch a two-dollar Nassau bet during regular weekend games with our buddies, the idea of performing heroically on the golf course in front of a gallery of thousands and a television audience of millions is staggering. Yet the world's top players not only function comfortably in that environment, the best of them rachet up their games a notch or two in the tensest of situations.

How is that possible? It must extend far beyond the fact that they are full-time golfers who hit thousands of balls in countless hours of practice, Hogan maintains. He believes they have managed to redirect their inner processes to accept the idea that high-pressure situations are indeed fun. Thus, pressure becomes a goal, a state to covet rather than avoid. "Good players have learned that pressure situations, stress-inducing situations, are good things, not bad," Hogan says. "It means they are in the chase, in the game, and for them that part is the fun part. Rather than avoid such stress, the best players seek it out week after week."

In 1979, Joseph Chilton Pearce published *The Magical Child*, which Hogan maintains is of utmost importance not only for golfers but for the planet itself. Pearce's book is an exploration of the developmental process of intelligence, from the fetus to the adult. Pearce writes that three billion years of mankind's evolution has equipped us with a mind and body capable of far more than we've ever imagined. But to progress, the human brain must first undergo stress, which allows the mind to tap its potential more deeply. This can be seen in the growth of intelligence in children, who move from the safety of the womb to the protection of the mother and later from the mother out into the world. Along the way, their intelligence increases in spurts that correspond to such stress factors. They often use play to explore their worlds and learn to draw on their innate intelligence and creativity to respond to that world.

Hogan sees our current culture as hostile to this magical child. First, western culture has suppressed our natural urge to be creative and use our sensory-based imagery in daily life. The Industrial Revolution, a memorization-based educational method, and even the Information Super Highway are all agents of the left brain's battle against creativity. At the same time, or perhaps as a result, the sense of safety children need is rapidly disappearing. Parents don't stay home as much to rear children, who now watch hours and hours of television. Our culture is fixated on content, consumerism, and collecting the most goods; it's also scary, scattered, and survivalist.

Seen in this light, Hogan believes that the mechanics-only teachers are not just screwing up millions of golfers, but are threatening the future of the planet itself! Even though we can see what the finest players in the world can achieve when they capture the twin feelings of security and playfulness on a golf course during a major tournament, the golfing world continues to be outcome-oriented, placing emphasis not on the game itself but on the final score.

Chuck Hogan sincerely believes golf may help save the planet. That is why he has volunteered much time and effort in recent years to help the LPGA's teaching division launch an inner-city youth golf program. The program began in East-Central Los Angeles and has now spread to other indigent urban areas. Relying on donations of golf equipment and play time at local public courses, the program teaches children of the ghetto and barrio how to swing a club and then lets them play.

"We give them three instructions," Hogan says. "Play fast, be courteous, and have fun. What else is there?" He says he has seen the program change young lives; the children discover there are environments and playgrounds far removed from the drug-infested, violent, hopeless streets of their worlds.

On the surface, at least, Chuck Hogan has always seemed to enjoy his position outside the mainstream of golf instruction. Indeed, he has been swimming upstream for more than twenty years now. It's certainly not always been an easy road. Like other iconoclasts, Hogan found himself cast as the outsider, at first derided and ignored then co-opted.

Early on, Hogan was denounced within the golf establishment as something of a nut. But when his professional clients began winning golf tournaments, having a coach who focused on the mental game suddenly became in vogue. Hogan has always simply called himself a golf instructor, but he launched the idea in golf of including a sports psychologist as part of one's entourage. Few touring pros are today without one.

Chuck Hogan has received at least one letter from a sports psychologist—one with the years of educational training that entitle him to use Dr. in front of his name—insisting that without the benefit of such an educational background, Hogan ought to desist from advising pro golfers. Outwardly he laughs off such critcism, but inwardly he seethes with the indignity of an intellectual accused of alchemy.

And, of course, Hogan's anti-mechanics cause is one that by nature is bound to rankle the golfing establishment. He is routinely ignored or slammed by the golfing press, especially the monthly magazines, because he continually rails against them for propagating the myth of the golf swing. The magazines make money selling tips du jour to the hordes of high handicap golfers desperate for a quick fix. Month after month, the magazines are glad to oblige. Although the establishment's hostility may not signal the worldwide conspiracy that Hogan hints at, it's true that if the golf magazines actually helped golfers get better, they would all go out of business.

Hogan has tried to fit in the best a square peg can ever fit into a round hole. But he still lurks on the outside of the establishment and seems content to stay there. He's never afraid to stand up and be counted as golf's leading contrarian. Listen, for instance, to his thoughts on the high priest of golf mechanics, Ben Hogan.

"I've never understood the myth that sprang up around Hogan," his no-relation namesake says. "First of all, his golf swing, about which everyone has always raved, was totally manufacturered; there was not a natural piece of Hogan's swing. Early in his career, Byron Nelson, for one, used to beat him up one side and down the other. And Hogan never was a good putter. Furthermore, he was not a nice man," Chuck Hogan goes on. "I mean look at all the power and influence Ben Hogan stored up as a role model and a golf hero. And what did he do with it? Nothing. What has he ever given back to the game of golf? This is supposed to be a great hero and role model? I don't get it at all."

Chuck Hogan doesn't get it, and many others don't get Chuck Hogan. Sounds like a draw.

Chuck Hogan

Practice Tee

The best mentally prepared golfers often utilize the concept of a D-line, or Decision line, when they are playing golf.

Draw an imaginary circle around the ball and make it big enough to include you within its confines, or simply imagine a line between you and the ball as you observe a shot from a down-the-line perspective.

Do not enter the circle or cross the D-line until you are absolutely positive regarding the shot you plan to execute and the destination of your ball. As you walk to the vicinity of the ball, you are scanning the target, its conditions, and the position of the ball. You take in variables of elevation, wind, distance, and more. Gather the yardage information and select a club appropriate for the shot you have envisioned.

Once you cross the line, you will execute the shot without hestitation and within a minimal time period.

There is no need to rush the shot, but you don't want to use more time than is necessary for your "go signal" to arise.

The entire reason for this routine is to be led to a go signal. Each step of the routine should amplify your preplanned decision of targeting your shot. Get excited and indulgent. Every shot is brand new. The fascinating quality of golf is that every shot is different.

—From *The Player's Course* by Chuck Hogan, S.E.A. 1991

Chapter Eight

SHELBY FUTCH

THE McDONALD'S PRINCIPLE

Shelby Futch got into golf because of a fortunate poker hand. Like Travis McGee, the fictional hero of John D. MacDonald's mystery series, who accepted a houseboat (named the *Busted Flush*) instead of cash for his poker winnings, Futch's father took home his opponent's golf clubs in exchange for money.

Futch was about ten years old at the time, living in the middle of west Texas, forty-eight miles north of Amarillo. His father worked for Continental Carpet, and the family lived in a company house and shopped at the company store. Continental Carpet built a squat nine-hole course for the employees, and that's where young Shelby broke in his father's poker winnings.

At first, he recalls, he didn't have any golf balls, so he whacked around a tennis ball. A year or so later, when his family moved to Oklahoma, his father bought him a golf ball. When Futch connected for the first time, he couldn't believe how far the ball flew. From that moment, he says, he was hooked on golf.

Futch never had a lesson as a youngster, but developed a natural swing that produced good results. He played in junior tournaments throughout Oklahoma, developing enough of a reputation in the state to earn a scholarship from Oklahoma State University.

But when he showed up on campus with his self-taught, unorthodox swing, the school's golf coach shook his head, telling Futch much work lay ahead. "He not only got me more orthodox in my swing," Futch recalls, "He got me to where I couldn't play a lick. I had to totally relearn the game, and I had a very hard time." Suffering through the trials of learning a new swing left Futch with an enduring sympathy for neophytes or those trying to correct faulty swings. "I don't think I would have been a good teacher if I hadn't had some disasters along the way and had to learn how to play again myself. It's not easy."

As a result of his struggles, Futch dropped out of golf and eventually out of college. Because it was the early 1960s, Uncle Sam tapped his shoulder, sending him to the army. He volunteered for everything, making his way through the airborne division to the Rangers, then to the special forces—the Green Berets.

As he moved up the ranks, Futch studied the way the army trained people to perform specific tasks in an overall framework. The army can quickly and efficiently train young men how to jump out of an airplane, pull the chute, land, and then survive once on the ground. The efficacy of military training methods impressed Futch immensely, and provided the model for his own teaching philosophies.

Futch noted that the army's method involved absolute organization—rehearsing, and re-rehearsing until everyone knew his place and knew his job. With the over-all framework predetermined and preplanned, and the personnel drilled to polished perfection, the result was usually ultimate performance. These were the lessons that Futch would later use in developing his chain of golf schools.

After his service in the armed forces, Futch returned to Oklahoma State still unsure what he wanted to do. He returned to golf to play tournaments, find new teachers, and begin to explore teaching himself. He spent several years seeking out the premiere teachers of the day, talking to them and observing their methods. Call it his scouting phase: observing, making notes, developing his own strategies. He filmed Claude Harmon giving a lesson at the Thunderbird Country Club in Palm Springs. "I wanted to see how they taught, figure out what they were seeing when they looked at a student," Futch says. "I would watch their eyes to see what they were looking at." However, he never discovered a single, comprehensive teaching strategy he could simply emulate. He also found that even the best teachers often had trouble articulating their philosophies.

Meanshile, his own game came back. He played on some tournament circuits for a while, including the Asian

Tour for a season or two. But he ran out of money while in Chicago, where he took a teaching job. Although his game was never good enough to beat the touring pros, he won the Illinois PGA championship as a club professional and was invited to the national PGA Championship at Firestone Country Club.

About this time, *Golf Digest* magazine launched its nationwide golf school program, using its teaching editors as instructors. The stable of teachers included well-known names like Bob Toski; Gardner Dickinson, a protégé of Ben Hogan; Harvey Penick from Texas; Ernie Vossler; Jim Flick; and a noted professional name from England, John Jacobs. Jacobs had been a successful tournament professional in Europe—former captain of the Ryder Cup and the Walker Cup teams—and had eventually turned to teaching, coaching some of Europe's best.

The magazine's instructional editor at the time, Cal Brown, was a friend of Futch's, and he invited Shelby to spend a week teaching a *Golf Digest* school with John Jacobs. "I did the school with John," Futch recalls. "And we got along great, just hit it off from the first moment. He didn't want to live over here, just come over and do five or six schools a year. He enjoyed teaching."

More importantly to Futch, John Jacobs was the first instructor he had encountered who could articulately describe the deficiencies he observed in a golf swing and his prescriptions for their correction. He possessed a rare eye for the golf swing that Futch greatly admired.

Golf Digest's main competitor, *Golf* magazine, soon decided to pursue its rival into the golf school business. It hired Cal Brown away from *Digest*, who recruited Jacobs and Futch to mastermind the new project, and the two men collaborated for about a year. Later, however, *Golf* magazine changed its mind dropping the program abruptly.

"I called John and said I think there's a different way to go, a different way to merchandise golf schools and a better way to set up a program," Futch recalls. "My idea was to make the schools less expensive and not so targeted just to the high-end user, the elite. I thought we should appeal to the masses, because it was obvious the game was going to the masses."

Futch knew that Jacobs had no desire to move to America and set up this new business, but he felt that Jacobs should play a part in the new enterprise, since many of the ideas of the instructional program he had in mind were Jacobs's. So the two cut a deal to form the John Jacobs Golf Schools: Shelby Futch would own and operate the business, and Jacobs would receive a royalty of sales. The partnership has endured more than twenty-five years, Futch says, with never a cross word. Although Jacobs has rarely taught in the school that carries his name, he and Futch have remained close, getting together with their families several times a year.

Still, because the namesake rarely makes appearances, something of a mystical aura has grown up around his name. "People always ask, 'Is there really a John

Jacobs?'" says Futch. "And I always say, 'Yeah, and he's doing a golf school today with Betty Crocker, Sara Lee, and Colonel Sanders!' But it's true that we've turned him into a brand name."

Because he planned from the outset to market his schools to average golfers, Futch knew he needed a simple message that most golfers could quickly assimilate. So he developed a standard teaching model that, he says, hasn't changed in twenty-five years. "Everybody writes articles about this new secret of golf or that new secret," Futch says. "I personally think the game hasn't changed dramatically in more than two hundred years. You have a club and a ball, and you stand to the side of it and try to hit it as far as you can. Equipment has changed and helped a bit, but the golf swing is still basically the same."

The teaching method the John Jacobs schools use has always focused on basics. Instructors are trained to ask and observe, "What is the ball doing?" From that question, the next follows: "What is the club doing to make the ball do that?" And finally, "What must the golfer then do to influence the golf club?"

It's a basic formula that boils down to fixing the impact point of each golfer's swing. If the golfer is slicing, the John Jacobs instructor shows him how to adjust the clubface back to the ball in a square or slightly closed position. By improving the impact point, one usually doesn't have to change the entire swing dramatically. And, conversely, if the impact is correct, the swing usually looks pretty good, and the student doesn't have to execute any complicated moves.

What is most interesting and unique about the John Jacobs schools is that Shelby Futch insists that his instructors be drilled in this method of teaching. No deviation from the model is allowed, although each instructor is permitted to put his personal touch on the program. Every two weeks, each John Jacobs instructor is filmed doing a five-minute presentation on the method, and Futch reviews each one to make sure the Jacobs line is being followed. "I remember an English teacher in college said, 'Let's take one of Shakespeare's sonnets and see if we can touch it up a little,'" Futch recalls. "So we'd go off for a week and try to improve it and come back and say, 'Gee, we can't improve this!' The professor would agree; Shakespeare's choice of words was that precise."

It is the same principle used by any major franchise organization, whether it be McDonald's or Holiday Inn or Wal-Mart. You can walk into any McDonald's in the country, order a Big Mac, and know exactly what you're going to get and how it's going to taste. Likewise, you can sign up at any John Jacobs Golf School and come away with the exact same golf instructional program. Franchisers call it quality control.

Futch demands the same precision of his teachers. The result is an organizational consistency that is most unusual. Futch says many students who return to the school after a first visit several years earlier note that they're being taught the same thing in the same way.

One student came back after fifteen years, he says, pulled out note cards from the first session, and compared the notes to the new lessons. They were the same.

This emphasis on consistency stems from Futch's military training: the teaching staff's constant, controlled, rehearsing mirrors his experience in the army—and produces the same efficient results. Even Futch himself toes the line. "I'm doing a clinic tomorrow for the Phoenix Suns," he says. "So I snuck out today for a few hours to rehearse my dialogue, make sure I had it all straight. And I've done this a jillion times!"

The Jacobs schools began in Tucson, Arizona, where Futch lived. After several years, the school outgrew its location at the Tucson National resort and moved north to Phoenix/Scottsdale, settling in at the Marriott Camelback resort. There, Futch met Roger Maxwell, the director of golf, who eventually rose to be golf director for the entire Marriott resort chain. Maxwell had built a large practice area and was trying to operate his own golf schools, but needed help.

Futch moved his operation in for a trial and immediately liked what he found. "Working with a hotel is like a three-legged stool," he says. "The three legs are the golf school, the golf course, and the hotel. If any of the three legs breaks down, the whole thing goes over. And Marriott was so consistent all the time."

That consistency of product appealed to Futch, who was trying to do the same in his golf schools. And he found great support not only from Maxwell, but from other Marriott executives. President Bill Marriott noticed that in his chain, which had average room night-stays of 2.8 nights, the John Jacobs Golf School was bringing in guests for six nights. Bill Marriott's retired father, J.W. Marriott, lived in Scottsdale and would occasionally drop into the Jacobs schools to listen to the presentation. The elderly Marriott noted with approval that the teaching message was consistent from one school and one week to the next.

With the support of Marriott, Futch began opening schools at other Marriott resorts around the country. When his customers from the eastern seaboard asked for locations closer to home, John Jacobs opened schools in Florida and the Southeast. Today, virtually every Marriott resort with a golf course is the site of a Jacobs school. It has been a partnership that has benefited both sides. In fact, Futch was an early buyer and is a longtime holder of Marriott stock, and he has profited handsomely over the years.

Although Bill Marriott has been supportive of the Jacobs programs, he is also the only student who has been to the school and never hit a golf ball. "He got a telephone call after about fifteen minutes and left," Futch laughs. "The man is going twenty-four hours a day!"

Futch says he never had a pro forma business plan and that his marketing concept was basic: provide the best golf instruction at the most reasonable price. At the same time, he strives to make the schools fun and interesting and to help his students improve. It's a simple formula, but then Wal-Mart's formula is equally simple: offer a wide variety of useful products at discounted prices. And like other well-run businesses, Futch pays attention to details. He works especially hard to make sure his staff of instructors continues to deliver the same, consistent message. In addition, students at John Jacobs schools are always asked to fill out comment cards, and Futch himself reads every one and personally calls any dissatisfied students.

While Futch never earned an MBA, or tried to, he has taken advantage of certain business synergies to help increase his bottom line. John Jacobs Golf Schools operates a travel division originally created to help students make travel arrangements to and from the schools. But some students would call back later asking for help planning a golf vacation to another resort or seeking Shelby's advice on good courses to visit. "I figured we might as well make it a full-service travel agency," Futch says, "especially since most general travel agents are not all that familiar with golf. It just fit together with what we were doing."

A second profit center is the company's custom club-making division. Students would frequently call asking if they should buy new clubs before coming to a school. Futch would tell them to wait, and the staff would measure and write custom specifications for the golfer at the school. "I had a background in club-making, and used to make and sell them when I was a pro in Chicago," he says. "I always believed one more blow with the hammer

would make me a great player!" So John Jacobs began fit-
ting students and making custom-fit clubs, filling a needed
niche in the market. And with the advent of cheaper
investment cast club technology, Jacobs could make clubs
of the same quality as those of the major brands—Wilson,
Spalding, Taylor Made, or Callaway. "That couldn't have
happened twenty-five years ago," Futch admits. "We'd
need a factory and trained people. But with today's marketplace, we can buy the components and custom assemble them here."

Now, Futch has purchased his own golf facility—
the Painted Mountain Golf Club in Mesa, Arizona, outside
Phoenix. "Everybody in golf secretly yearns to own his
own club," Futch smiles. With twenty-seven holes of golf,
and a huge new practice facility that runs 270 degrees and
contains six greens, numerous bunkers, sidehill areas, and
more, plus a Rodeway Inn down the street, Futch is in
control of his golf students from dawn to dusk.

Focused on his goal of teaching the masses, Shelby
Futch has never pursued opportunities to instruct high
profile professional golfers. He says he dislikes the attention, the glare of publicity, that accompanies that kind of
teaching. "I don't feel comfortable with that," he says. "I
don't like to go to tournaments and stand around on the
practice tee. That doesn't appeal to me at all. I have
worked with some players, and will watch someone if
they ask me, but I've always felt like I'm taking some of
their shine." Perhaps he's also been affected by something
Harvey Penick told him many years ago. When Futch

asked Penick what he told his two prize students, Ben Crenshaw and Tom Kite, Penick admitted, "I don't tell 'em very much—I'm afraid to tell them too much, afraid to mess them up!"

Indeed, Futch receives hundreds of resumés from golf professionals every year seeking to join his 110-member staff. And whenever he sees one of those golf professionals state as their career goal "to be the world's greatest teacher," he files it in the OUT basket. "That's not the kind of person I want in my school," he says. "I want someone who says they enjoy teaching and who can organize all the students and kick all the rocks out of the way, so they can really do their trade, which is to teach."

In the end, that is what Shelby Futch and his John Jacobs Golf Schools do, and they do it for more than 12,000 students every year in more than 1,000 class sessions. With all the non-glamour of a Big Mac with cheese, Futch and his well-trained staff impart their simple messages to their grateful students who, at least for a little while, can hit the ball straighter, longer, and better.

Although no blond golfing god will ever step to the podium at the U.S. Open and publicly thank Shelby Futch for getting him to the pinnacle, Futch is very satisfied helping instead the 12,000 choppers and hackers who truly appreciate not slicing or topping anymore after a John Jacobs session. Futch is also getting rich as a result of his choice to serve the masses rather than the glamorous few. There will always be an almost limitless supply of high handicap golfers. "I used to worry about paying for my kids' educations and orthodontist bills and such," Futch says. "Then I'd go sit on a bench at a golf course and watch people try to hit a golf ball and feel instantly okay again! And especially because I know you can help them instantly, and they'll go, 'WOW!' like I pulled a rabbit out of the hat."

SHELBY FUTCH

PRACTICE TEE

For years, tour players have maintained that a normal greenside bunker shot is one of the easiest in the game. Most weekend golfers would disagree. They fear the shot. However, if you can learn the correct method and are prepared to practice it, you can quickly make yourself into a good sand player.

The Splash Shot: The prime objective in playing from a good lie is to slide the clubface under the ball, taking a fairly shallow cut of sand. To do that, the clubface of the sand wedge must be open to some degree so that the back of the sole strikes the sand first, creating a skidding or sliding effect (commonly referred to as bounce). With the face square, the club digs too deeply.

When you open the clubface, aiming the leading edge to the right of target, the ball will fly to the right unless you compensate by swinging to the left of the target. To set this up, align your feet and shoulders to the left of target, positioning the ball forward in the stance, and keeping your weight evenly balanced on both feet.

Aim to enter the sand about two inches behind the ball (however, the bounce of the club will allow you to hit up to four inches behind the ball and the club will still skid through). Now, swing along your shoulder line, cutting across the ball from out to in, and the ball will fly straight at the target. Make a point of swinging fully back and through with a complete unwinding of the hips through impact. Full power is not necessary, so feel the correct speed with a couple of practice swings outside the bunker.

Chapter Nine

PEGGY KIRK BELL

RIDING THE WOMEN'S WAVE

In her seventeenth summer, Peggy Kirk of Finley, Ohio, was told by her mother that she was too old to go to summer camp. She had just graduated from Finley High School, and her mother insisted she go to college in the fall.

"But what am I going to do this summer?" the young girl wailed. "I don't know," her mother answered, "But you're staying home."

One can easily imagine the teenager rushing up, flinging herself on her bed, and thinking hateful thoughts about mean old parents. But Peggy's problem was solved almost immediately. "The Lord just had a map for me," she says today.

The very next day a man walked into Peggy's father's office, said he was being transferred and needed to get rid of his membership bond in the Finley Country Club, and asked if Mr. Kirk would be interested. The membership cost $100, which in the Depression years of the early 1930s was a hefty sum. At first Mr. Kirk refused, telling the man that neither he nor his wife played that silly game of golf. "Perhaps your children?" the man suggested. Recalling his daughter pouting at home, Peggy Kirk's dad forked over the C-note and became a member of the club.

In short order, Peggy Kirk laid her hands on a ragged collection of golf clubs: a three-wood; three-, five-, seven-, and nine-irons; and a putter. She found three old balls and marched off to the Finley club to try out this new game.

"I marched up, didn't know a thing," she recalls. "I said, 'Where do you start?' They pointed out the first tee." She teed up her first ball, and gripping her club "like a baseball bat," swung from the heels. "I never made it to the first green," she laughs. "I hit all three of my balls into the woods, and because I was new, I didn't stop to see where the balls went. So I lost all three."

Undeterred, the young lady entered the pro shop and asked, "Who's the teacher here?" The man behind the counter asked if she would like a lesson. "Yeah!" the girl nodded eagerly. "Fine," the man said. "Meet me here tomorrow morning at nine o'clock and bring fifty cents for the lesson."

Peggy was taken aback. Tomorrow? She wanted to learn today! And fifty cents per lesson? Where was she going to get that kind of money? In fact, where was she going to get some new golf balls?

But the youngster was determined, so she showed up bright and early the next morning for her first lesson with Finley's head professional, Leonard Smutty. In that first meeting, Smutty showed her how to grip the club properly and watched her hit a few balls. Peggy was a tall, athletic girl with broad shoulders and unusual strength. Following the lesson, the pro asked the girl how serious she was about learning golf.

"It's all I have to do this summer," she replied. "Okay," Smutty said. "I'll help you as long as you work at it." For the rest of the summer, Peggy Kirk was the first person to arrive at the golf course. She constantly practiced under Smutty's watchful eye. "I'd be hitting balls over there while he gave someone else a lesson. Then, between lessons, he'd come over and talk to me," she recalls. "He was a good friend. Leonard played on the Tour himself early in his career. He traveled the road with Horton Smith in an old rickety car. He was a good player who led the first round of the U.S. Open one year. But then he got married and had a family and stayed put in Finley. And I'm lucky he did, because he helped motivate me to get into golf."

Peggy picked the game up quickly and learned how to hit the ball a long way. She began competing in the club's ladies' day events, soon moving on to the Toledo district's amateur competitions. The entire Toledo area was a hotbed of tournament golf. Byron Nelson served as head professional at Inverness. Frank Stranahan, another nationally renowned player, was a Toledan, as was Barbara McIntire, who was about ten years younger than Peggy Kirk.

Her father, who had almost accidentally introduced her to golf, was delighted to see young Peggy blossom in the sport. During her high school years, the tomboyish and athletic girl had wistfully contemplated playing professional baseball someday. So the elder Kirk spared no expense for his young golf prodigy; she soon had a set of Kenneth Smith custom-made clubs and never had to scrounge around for balls again.

Peggy Kirk became a fine amateur player, first in Ohio and then on the national stage. Of course, in the 1930s and early 1940s there was no professional tour for women. Nevertheless, the amateurs offered a long summer schedule of tournaments all over the country.

Then Babe Didrickson Zaharias came along. The great Babe had shone brightly in the 1932 Olympic Games, becoming one of the most popular celebrities of her day. After experimenting with several sports, the Babe settled on golf, initially as a professional playing exhibitions against men for money. She later applied to the U.S. Golf Association for reinstatement as an amateur and played alongside Peggy Kirk on the circuit. She later grew bored and resumed her professional status.

After the second world war, Babe Zaharias was one of the few athletes, and the only woman, who could command appearance fees exceeding $1,000 for a golf exhibition or match against a local hero. Among golfers, only

Byron Nelson, Ben Hogan, and Sam Snead could do the same.

When Babe decided to turn professional again in 1947, there were only a handful of professional tournaments for women on the schedule: the Texas Open, the Western Open, the Titleholders, and the U.S. Women's Open, which did not begin until 1946. To remedy this situation, Babe Zaharias and her manager, Fred Corcoran, would book an exhibition match for the normal fee of $1,000 and then suggest that the local sponsor "put on a tournament for women." She convinced the sponsors to use her fee as the basis for a tournament purse and promised to provide the competitors.

That's where Peggy Kirk came in. Her friend Babe urged her in 1947 to turn pro and join the fledgling circuit. Peggy resisted. "I asked her why I should turn pro when there was no place for pros to play!" Peggy recalls. "I said I like to play golf. Well, Babe said we're gonna make it big. And we made it big!"

Babe talked most of the best women amateurs into joining the new Ladies Professional Golf Tour: Louise Suggs, Jackie Pung, Betsy Rawls, and Betty Hicks. Corcoran signed on new sponsors and new tournaments and Babe brought her friends in to play. In the earliest days, there were perhaps eight touring professionals, and the rest of the field was drawn from the best amateur women in the area where the tournament was held.

Peggy joined the circuit in the fall of 1950 as a

charter member of the LPGA. In the early days, life on the tour was one constant barnstorming promotion. One of Corcoran's early sponsors was Alvin Hanmacher, who owned a New York dress-making firm. Hanmacher formed the Weathervane Team to help promote his line of women's suits. "Every girl on tour had these suits," Peggy recalls. "We'd go up to New York and pick up as many as we wanted! I must have had thirty Hanmacher suits—dressy ones and tailored ones. I always wore a Hanmacher suit and one of their scarfs with roosters on them."

In fact, Hanmacher sponsored a team of LPGA pros who went abroad to compete against an English team of women in an international competition that far predates today's Solheim Cup. The players on the U.S. team gained points based on their performance during the short LPGA season. "There were five tournaments, beginning in Miami and working across to Dallas," Peggy recalls. "In addition to playing, all the girls would go to all the stores, like Neiman-Marcus, and stand there in our Hanmacher suits. All of us!"

Peggy barnstormed and played the tour for about three years before she ran into an old schoolmate back home in Ohio. Warren "Bullet" Bell had been a noted high school athlete in Finley. Although she never dated him in high school, Peggy does remember when Bell sent her a note in the third grade saying, "Do you love me or Duane Hindell?" She wrote him back, "I love you both." Unfortunately, the teacher intercepted the missive, and Peggy fled the room in tears.

But she bumped into Bullet Bell again after he returned from Korea as a wounded veteran, and he confronted her. "Hey, I hear you're a hot-shot golfer," she remembers his opening challenge. "I'll bet I can beat you!" They arranged a game for the wager of a movie date. Bell, although not lacking in cockiness, had never played golf before. "So he took me to the movies," Peggy said, "And that was the beginning of our romance."

Peggy had signed a contract with Spalding, through the efforts of Babe Zaharias, and Spalding sold her name to Sears, Roebuck & Co. As a result, Peggy Kirk Bell toured the country when she wasn't playing in tournaments, giving clinics at Sears stores. "I must have given a clinic in every Sears store or parking lot from coast to coast selling Spalding clubs," she remembers. "But that's how you made your money as a pro. I made about $10,000 a year doing that, and that was pretty good money."

It was certainly better than teaching school, which she had contemplated doing after college. She had majored in physical education, and the plan was to teach in junior high. But after earning her degree, she spent a few months practice-teaching and never went back. "The girls in the class didn't want to do anything. They didn't want to run or exercise. They just wanted to look pretty," Peggy recalls. "That was the era, of course. And I ended up having to teach the boys' classes too, because all the coaches were over in Korea in the army. My first teaching job would have paid around $3,000 a year. I said forget this and went back to golf."

As a barnstorming pro, giving clinics for Spalding at Sears stores, Peggy got her first experience demonstrating the golf swing. "It was pretty basic stuff then," she says. "I just demonstrated how I did it. I showed them how I grip the club, turn and unturn, wind and unwind, and never hit the ball, just swing the club. It's the same thing I teach today."

Peggy reached something of a crossroads in her life in 1953. That was the year she and Bullet Bell married and purchased a golf course in Southern Pines, North Carolina, just down the road from Pinehurst.

Warren Bell, an all-state, three-sport letterman in high school and at Ohio State, had been drafted and sent to Korea, returning with an injured shoulder. Still, he played three years in the National Basketball Association, for Fort Wayne, Indiana. But his shoulder got worse, and he had to quit. He began looking around for a golf course to buy, figuring that would be a good business for him and his star wife.

In 1953, Warren and Peggy Bell bought a third interest in the Pine Needles golf course along with PGA Tour player Julius Boros and the Cosgrove family of Pinehurst. Boros was married to a Cosgrove daughter at the time. The golf course, designed by Pinehurst resident and noted architect Donald Ross, was once part of a lovely golf resort in Southern Pines. But the Depression had hit the area hard, and the elegant brick hotel had been sold to the Roman Catholic church and converted to a hospital.

The church hadn't wanted the golf course, so a local man had leased it for a dollar a year. After five years of struggle, he had also decided to get out. The Cosgroves, who owned the Mid Pines Inn across the street, wanted to buy the course. With the help of son-in-law Boros, who was playing regularly on the PGA Tour, and with Warren Bell to manage the facility, the deal was done.

Within two years, however, the deal changed. Julius Boros' wife died suddenly, and he decided to move to Florida to escape the memories. So Warren Bell raised $50,000 and bought out the other two interests in the golf course. He then acquired some land at the end of the first hole envisioned for a rustic golf lodge in the pines. Almost singlehandedly, Bullet Bell drew up the plans, hired the plumbers and carpenters, and created the Pine Needles Lodge.

Peggy Bell was right there by her husband's side the whole time. She became pregnant with their first child, Bonnie, in 1954 and thereafter became a part-time LPGA player. The Bells not only raised three kids together, but developed a healthy business as well. "I remember we had the first showers in the Pinehurst area," Peggy says. "Everyone else had tubs on legs with curtains. We had the first air-conditioned rooms and the first swimming pool in the area. When we first arrived in town, I had to take the kids down to some dirty old lake in Aberdeen to go swimming."

As the resort began to grow, Peggy Kirk Bell found herself taking up a new profession: golf teacher. It began when the Bells were still just operating the golf course, before they began building the resort. One day a woman walked into the pro shop and asked for a lesson. "Bullet looked at me and said, 'Go give her a lesson'," Peggy remembers. "I said 'I'm not a teacher!' And he said, 'Well you know more than she does, so go tell her something!'"

Peggy's first lesson was not a great success. She showed her pupil how to grip the club and a few other basics, and the woman began hacking at the ball. "Every time she'd miss one, I'd tell her do this or do that! I got so frustrated because nothing was working that I must have kept her on the tee for three hours! She finally looked up at me and pleaded, 'Can I quit, now?' I said, 'But you're not hitting it yet!' I couldn't understand why she couldn't hit the ball. I've always wondered if that woman quit golf for good after my lesson!"

Things did not improve at first. Old-time members at Pine Needles can still remember how she would tell students to go away, practice something and not come back until they had mastered it. "That's how I got rid of them," she admits with a laugh. "I was still thinking I could win the Open or play more on tour, and I wanted to work on my own game. These people would keep coming up and asking for lessons, but I didn't want to give any!"

A year later she was pregnant again and even more motivated to cut down on her time on the lesson tee. So she raised her rates from three dollars an hour to five dollars. Her lesson book filled up at a faster rate! So she raised her fee again, this time to ten dollars. People continued to request lessons. "I didn't know what was going on," she says. "I didn't really want to teach, I wanted to play. But when they kept signing up and calling, well, then it became a challenge to me to do it better."

And fate intervened again. Bullet Bell had the first of a series of heart attacks that forced him to limit his involvement with the resort's business operations. And Peggy had two more children, which cut down the time she had to compete on Tour. Her life had changed, and as her roles as a mother and a partner in a business began demanding more of her time and attention, she changed with it. She learned that teaching could be fun and rewarding as long as she did not expect her students to begin playing as well as she could after one lesson. She began to think more about the golf swing and her theories on it and how to best communicate them to others.

"I had a friend who taught a lot," Peggy says. "He said first and foremost you have to make sure they have the right grip. But I've found it's no fun just working on the grip all the time."

Peggy Bell has learned that the most important part of teaching is initially sizing up a student: learning what they want out of golf and understanding their limitations.

"I always find out how much they're going to work and practice," she says. "If they are just occasional players, I know I'm not going to give them a lot of hard work to do, just some hints and tips to make certain shots easier."

But Bell is a believer in the golf swing, and her main goal is to make students understand what a golf swing is and what it isn't. "If you can make them understand what a golf swing is and what they need to do, they start to understand what they need to try and do to make changes. That's much more helpful than standing out on the range hitting ball after ball," she says.

Both Peggy and Warren Bell understood that golfers strive to improve—it's a central mission of the game— which is why they invested in building an extensive practice range facility at Pine Needles. When they first bought the golf course, the practice area extended barely 180 yards, ending in a narrow creek. Before the age of the Environmental Protection Agency and the need for exhaustive environmental studies, the Bells cleared some land next to the creek, moved its banks several hundred yards away and created a new range area. After installing two-sided tees and covered hitting areas to protect against inclement weather, they added a variety of chipping greens and practice bunkers.

As Peggy Kirk Bell's reputation as a teacher grew and blossomed, they began marketing instruction-oriented "Golfaris" at Pine Needles, including a handful a year for women only. And, just as in the early days when Peggy tried to avoid lessons by raising the rates, people have flocked to get in. The Pine Needles Golfaris are extremely popular and annually over-subscribed.

A typical Golfari runs for a week and has 140 students. Peggy's widespread reputation as a fine teacher and genuine person attracts guest instructors from the ranks of LPGA's teaching division, college coaches, and others to form a faculty of twenty-six for a typical Golfari.

"Our students leave with a good understanding of their golf swings, and if they don't it's their own fault!" Peggy laughs. "We work two-and-a-half hours in the morning and afternoon, and they go play the golf course. Then, from four to six in the afternoon, it's open range time, and the instructors are there to work on specific problems. And the fun we have is unbelievable. At night, with all those gals, the place is rockin'! We get groups from country clubs who come together, and even the staff scrambles every year so they can come join the fun."

Despite the popularity of her Golfaris, Peggy Bell limits them to just seven a year, usually in the spring and fall. "Otherwise we'd be having them all the time," she says. "And it becomes a problem getting a good staff together for too many." In the summer months, the resort runs golf camps for juniors, which Peggy enjoys tremendously. Very likely, they stir powerful memories for her of that seventeen-year-old girl who first learned how to grip a club back in 1920s Finley, Ohio.

"This year we had one of our women's Golfaris, and as usual, I went right down the line with my clipboard to see all the students hitting, taking some notes on what to do with 'em," she says. "I saw this one little old lady struggling, and thought, gee, you've gotta help her! Well, she looked over at me and said, 'You know, Peggy, you and I are the same age.' I was aghast! I took my clipboard and wrote a note to my daughter who was working with the next student down: 'Number B-10 is my age—I'm going home to take a nap!'"

Over the years, teaching thousands of golfers, Peggy Bell has noted some differences, especially between male and female golfers. "Women listen better and they don't try to hit it so hard," she says succinctly. "Men want to hit the ball so hard. And most of them don't want to practice something—they're looking for the quick fix."

Peggy preaches the golf swing, not the golf hit. "It's like a ballet," she says, "a beautiful flowing motion. It's not beating at that little ball all tight with tension. I think that golfers should practice swinging more instead of just beating balls. If you develop a good, rhythmic swing, you'll become a better golfer and enjoy the game more within your limitations."

She recalls once suggesting that a female student just do practice swings, staying in balance and holding the finish. She left the woman on the tee swinging and swinging. The next afternoon, Peggy came upon the woman again, still swinging and swinging. "Good!" Peggy told her. "How's the ball doing?" The woman said, "I haven't hit one yet!" She'd been swinging without a ball for two days! Peggy had her put a ball down on the tee and the woman cracked it 210 yards.

Peggy Bell is also a believer in both mimicry and demonstration. She likes to physically put a golfer in the right positions at points during the swing so they can feel the proper position. "I'll take the club back for them and let them feel it," she says. "Then do it again and again." The schools use all the usual drills and teaching aids, but it's all working for a common goal: to reprogram a student's mind to the right sequence of motion and help them understand that process. "It's a game of feel," she maintains. "To hit the ball well is easy as long as the swing is flowing."

Peggy Kirk Bell's life in golf has flowed with the same grace and elegance she wants her students to adopt in their swings. Not that there haven't been patches in the rough. Warren Bell died of cancer at age 63. "I was so fortunate that I married a guy who loved the game as much as I did," she remembers wistfully. "He went out and shot a 71 on Friday and died on Monday. He said, 'Just when I got this damn game figured out!'"

Bullet Bell loved Pine Needles, but because of his ill health he had considered selling the resort before he died. Peggy talked him out of it, "I said my kids love this place."

All the Bell children are still involved in the family business. Eldest daughter Bonnie works in administration, and her husband, former PGA Tour player Pat McGowan, assists Peggy with the golf school. Peggy Ann tutors at the Golfaris and organizes the summer youth camps. Her husband, Kelly, is an accomplished amateur player in Carolina circles and is general manager of the resort. Peggy's son, Kirk, is in the mortgage banking business in Pinehurst ("we call him Mr. Cash," his mother laughs), and his wife Holly heads the resort's sales department.

All of Peggy's children are golfers. Bonnie competed for North Carolina, Peggy Ann and Kirk at Alabama. "All three were good players," their mother says. "Bonnie I think could have gone on to the pros, but she married Pat and quit." Peggy is quietly encouraging son-in-law Pat McGowan to consider tackling the PGA Tour again. "I tell him he's too good not to try," she says. "But he got kind of burned out, and it's no fun losing your card. He likes being home, teaching, and not worrying about missing putts!"

And the business continues to grow. A few years ago, the Bell family purchased the Mid Pines Resort across the street from Pine Needles, along with its Donald Ross-designed golf course. That resort features a sprawling, old-fashioned hotel that dates back to the Golden Age of hospitality, when the Pinehurst area was a winter playground for wealthy golfers from the Northeast, and the reclamation project has been an expensive one. The hotel needed almost complete refurnishing and new windows, and the golf course was in bad shape, too.

"When the Cosgroves bought Mid Pines back in the 1950s, they paid $120,000 for it," Peggy remembers. In the 1970s, they sold it to Quality Inn for $1,025,000. Warren and I had bid $1,020,000 for it, but he was ill and we had already built our hotel by then. I can't tell you how many more millions we paid for it this time!"

Now another major project is occupying the family's time: preparing for the 1996 U.S. Women's Open. The U.S. Golf Association, mindful of the role Peggy Kirk Bell has played in the history of women's golf as first a player and then a nurturer of players, awarded the tournament to Pine Needles. It even shifted the dates of the tournament from their traditional July to the first week in June to avoid the usual punishing heat and humidity of the North Carolina summer.

Peggy Kirk Bell is excited that the world of women's golf is coming to call at her home. But she's even more excited about the future of women's golf. She notes the teen girls that sign up for her summer camp and the number of executive women who are taking up the game. "It's amazing how many women are playing," she says. "I think it's great."

PEGGY KIRK BELL

PRACTICE TEE

Ladies tend to fear hitting out of heavy rough. Here are some points to remember when faced with such a shot:

1. If you have a long distance to go, be sure you have a seven-wood. Otherwise, use a lofted iron and just get the ball back onto the fairway.

2. Open the clubface a little.

3. Play the ball back in your stance.

4. Pick the club up sharply on the backswing.

5. Move the weight aggressively to the left leg on the downswing.

6. Hit down abruptly on a steep angle of approach, trying to hit the ball first and not the grass behind the ball.

7. Remember, if the ball is hit well, it will run a great deal after it lands.

Chapter Ten

JIMMY BALLARD

THE BABE RUTH CONNECTION

Jimmy Ballard was once the hottest teaching professional in the country. Every touring pro who came to see him quickly began winning money and tournaments. And then—pfffft!—it was gone, leaving Ballard wandering through the wilderness, shut out of the spotlight of fame. And now, in that peculiar circle of fate, he's back full force, coaching pros to victory.

What caused this cycle of fame, oblivion, and fame again for the down-home Alabama boy? Was it a kind of establishment conspiracy against the rebel with a cause? Or just the way things happened?

Jimmy Ballard was born in Carollton, Georgia, but grew up in Gadsden, Alabama. He took up golf early, encouraged by a family friend, and became quite proficient as a junior player. In 1956, he captured the Alabama Junior championship at fourteen. His style was of the John

Daly school—rear back and rip it—but he found he could play well, beating even older competitors.

Later that year his family moved to Birmingham. His father, an executive with the Kroger grocery store chain, had to relocate every few years to take over a new territory. When Ballard arrived in Birmingham and enrolled in Woodlawn High School there, he found that few of his peers were into golf. They deeply favored football and basketball: the school, three thousand students strong, was perennial state champion in those sports.

So Ballard tucked his clubs away in the closet, focusing instead for the next three years football and basketball, and baseball in the spring—at least before spring practice began on the gridiron.

But in his senior year, Ballard tore up a knee playing football, missing the basketball season because of his injury. Forced into athletic idleness, he decided to dig out his golf clubs. The first time he teed a ball up, Ballard shot a 69. "I thought, man, this is gonna be a breeze!" he laughs today. It wasn't. He shot scores in the 80s and 90s as often as the 70s. After he started reading golf magazines and seeking lessons from club professionals in the Birmingham area, his scores ballooned even higher. He remembers, "I had to chip in to break 80."

One day he picked up a game with Lee Mackay, another fine Alabama player who had known Ballard in his younger heydays. Mackay watched, appalled, as Ballard shot an 81 and asked, "Son, what the hell have you done to your golf swing?" Ballard began reciting the tips he had gleaned from his many lessons and the golf magazines, and Mackay replied, "Naw, that stuff's all wrong. You used to have such a nice natural swing. I'm taking you to see Sam Byrd."

Sam Byrd had started his athletic career in baseball, playing for the New York Yankees from 1929 to 1936, alongside such stalwarts as Babe Ruth (with whom he roomed on the road), Lou Gehrig, and the rest of Murderer's Row. After his baseball career, Byrd had moved into golf, accumulating twenty-five tournament victories on the Tour. In 1945, the year Byron Nelson steamrollered the Tour with his eleven straight tournament titles, Sam Byrd was often his bird-dog, finishing second to Nelson several times, including the '45 PGA Championship. Byrd finished second at the Masters in 1941 and '42 as well.

After his playing days, Byrd became head golf professional at the Anniston Country Club in Alabama, and by the time young Jimmy Ballard sought his counsel, he was managing a driving range in the Crestwood neighborhood in Birmingham. The two hit it off immediately, and Jimmy was soon employed by Mister Sam as an assistant. There he first encountered Byrd's theories on connection, and they have remained Ballard's central teaching thesis ever since.

Sam Byrd had been a student of how to hit a baseball when he was with the Yankees, scrutinizing the swings of all the great hitters (including his roomie, the Great Bambino) searching for common characteristics. What Babe Ruth showed the kid from Alabama was that all great hitters could tuck a towel under the armpit of their leading side (left or right) and hold it there throughout the swing. To hit a baseball without dropping the towel, of course, meant that the leading arm had to be kept tucked in against the body. As a result, the body and shoulders—not just the arms and hands—had to turn through and into the ball.

That was the basis for Byrd's theory of connection: using the large muscle groups of shoulders, torso, and legs to create the swing, rather than the thin muscles of the hands and arms. Its genesis was with the great Babe Ruth.

Interestingly, Babe Ruth would take Sam Byrd out to the golf course on off days. Ruth, as is well known, was an avid golfer. But Bambino mythology holds that he was a monstrously long hitter of the golf ball, which, Byrd confided to Ballard, was not true. Ruth was a talented player, but his strengths were chipping and putting. In fact, although he swung hard at the ball, he was not overly long off the tee.

Byrd found it very interesting when Ruth gave him golf pointers, telling him to keep his left arm straight and the swing upright. Byrd realized that they were just the opposite of the swing tips Ruth had given him on the diamond; and he instinctively knew that if he tried to hit a baseball with a stiff left arm, he would pop out every time.

So Byrd tucked a handkerchief under his left arm and began to swing at the golf ball trying to keep it there. The towel method had helped him learn how to swing level at a baseball. Now, instead of a horizontal swing plane, he tilted it to hit the ball on the ground and did the same thing. It worked well enough for Byrd to enjoy a fine career as a professional golfer. During that career, the popular sportswriter Grantland Rice asked Byrd if he'd like to collaborate on a golf instruction book on the Sam Byrd method, explaining the difference between his baseball swing and his golf swing. Byrd looked at the writer and said, "Granny, in baseball, I held a towel under my left armpit and got the bat right here and right there. In golf, I held a handkerchief under my left armpit, changed my plane, and got the club right here and right there. Granny, it's going to be a damn short book, ain't it?"

When Byrd left baseball and joined the fledgling pro golf tour, he came under the influence of Wild Bill Melhorn. "I made a golfer out of Sam Byrd," Melhorn once claimed. "There wasn't one shot in golf that I didn't talk to Sam about how he could do it the same as if it was in baseball. Like throwing underhanded across the body or sidearmed, which is the way you swing a golf club."

It became the one fundamental that Byrd taught to all his students once he became a club pro. Among these students, Ballard claims, was one of the greatest golfers of all time: Ben Hogan. Early in his career, Hogan almost starved to death as a golf professional. A notorious hooker, he constantly fought a tendency to come over the top of the ball.

"Hogan's old swing was strictly straight-left-arm stuff," Ballard says. "That stiff left arm disconnected, and when he came through, his right arm was under the left, he flicked his hands, and hit the duck hook. He called it the terror of the field mice."

Ballard recalls Hogan's fateful session with Byrd in 1945, when Byrd taught him the handkerchief-under-the-armpit swing. Suddenly, Hogan got his shoulders involved in the swing, which helped his head, eyes, and spine make the move that Ballard says all the great golfers make. And the rest, as they say, is history.

That move, the common denominator for greatness, runs contrary to the two most common swing instructions most golfers learn: "Keep your head down," and "Keep your left arm straight." With the connection swing, says Ballard, the left arm does not stay straight but bends gently around the chest. Keeping that arm connected to the torso while it coils in behind the ball makes the spine shift laterally behind the ball during the backswing and forward again on the throughswing. And since the head is connected to the spine, it too shifts back or right on the backswing and forward on the downswing.

"You can look at the photos and videos of all the great players in history," Ballard says, as he pulls out his bulging notebooks of swing photos. "When they were playing their best golf, none of them kept their head frozen over the ball, and none of them had a stiff left arm. They all shift into the right place (in the backswing), and their left arm lies next to their breast. They can all hold a handkerchief under their armpits. Look at Jack Nicklaus; he never held his head still over the ball. In fact, he initiated his swing by cocking his head back to the right. All those years everybody saw that, and they still said Nicklaus holds his head still! Hogan shifted his head, too, as did Hal Sutton. Sam Snead and Curtis Strange moved their heads back with their spines. All the good players did it."

In 1965, Sam Byrd accepted another club professional position and sold his interest in the Birmingham driving range and teacher center to his young disciple. Ballard continued teaching the Byrd method and developed quite a reputation in local circles as someone who could help both hackers and seasoned players alike. In 1972, Ballard moved to the Pine Harbor Country Club, a financially troubled resort, golf club, and marina in Pell City, Alabama, about fifty miles from Birmingham. One of the original investors who had developed Pine Harbor was Paul "Bear" Bryant, the University of Alabama's god-like football coach. Ballard and a partner purchased the resort, and his career kicked into high gear.

While Ballard was Byrd's assistant in Birmingham, a young PGA Tour pro named Dewitt Weaver Jr. stopped in for lessons. Weaver recommended Ballard to a friend on the Tour, Mac McLendon, who visited Ballard in 1972 at Pine Harbor. "Mac was a good player when he first went out on the Tour," Ballard says. "I think he finished second in his first tournament, and then his swing went bad on him and he struggled for a couple of years." Ballard introduced him to Byrd's connection theories, coaching him for a few weeks before sending McLendon back out on Tour. McLendon eventually triumphed in five PGA Tour tournaments before retiring. "He never really wanted to stay out there for a long career," Ballard says. "He studied to be a stockbroker and began to raise his family."

But Ballard's success with McLendon did not go unnoticed in the locker rooms of the Tour, and soon a long line of pros began to form at the front door of Pine Harbor. Jim Colbert became a client. So did J.C. Snead, Leonard Thompson, Bobby Walzel, and others. Johnny Miller studied with Ballard for a time, as did Gary Player. Later, LPGA pros came, as do Senior Tour pros today. Ballard was recognized as the swing guru of the 1970s and early 1980s. Only Jimmy Ballard really knows for sure which, and how many, pros came calling. "The list is more than two hundred and counting," Ballard estimates with a wistful smile.

In 1981 Ballard and his partner sold Pine Harbor, and Ballard was recruited by the owners of the Doral Resort and Country Club in Miami to establish a golf school program. He spent eight years in Miami, while the parade of PGA Tour stars continued. Ballard was a hot property. His theory of connection was discussed in the major golf magazines, he wrote his book *How to Perfect Your Golf Swing*, and he made several instructional videos.

Among his stable of Tour players were two shooting stars: Hal Sutton and Curtis Strange. Ballard began tutoring Sutton, a country boy from the deep South, long before he entered the Tour in 1982. His debut was stunning. In his second year on Tour, he won the Players Championship and the PGA Championship, and led the money list with $426,668. Considered one of the best ball-strikers on Tour, he was heralded as the second coming of the man he beat at Riviera Country Club to win that PGA: Jack Nicklaus. He enjoyed four more excellent seasons after that one, but when he left Ballard in 1988, he dropped to 88th on the money list and struggled for the next several years. His last win was in 1986.

Curtis Strange began working closely with Jimmy Ballard in 1980, spending nine years under his wing. In those nine years, Strange accumulated sixteen of his seventeen career victories, led the PGA Tour's money-winning list three times, and captured his back-to-back U.S. Opens in 1988 and '89. When he left Ballard, his winning days ended as well; Strange has not won on tour since 1989.

Although Ballard's star students were racking up wins and banking huge amounts of cash even as other PGA Tour players continued to come calling, Ballard began to feel that something wasn't right. He now believes that he suffered a backlash from other teachers, from the PGA teaching ranks, and even from Tour players jealous of his students' successes.

The period when Ballard was king of the hill mysteriously gave way to a bitter time when his theories came under attack. He was, after all, alone in teaching a technique that directly contradicted most others'. His ideas about the left arm, moving the head, and coiling behind the ball instead of turning the shoulders were all considered radical. Other teachers began to criticize Ballard's ideas, and the students—both professional and amateur—

who carried his lessons out into the real world found that no one else would validate Ballard's theories.

Sutton was perhaps the first victim to fall prey to this campaign against Ballard. Sutton's peers insisted that he couldn't win over the long term with Ballard's odd swing. "He teaches a sway," said the wags on the practice tees of the Tour. "Nobody can win consistently with a sway." Despite the evidence piling up with compound interest in his bank accounts, Sutton, young and impressionable, was persuaded by such arguments. And, Sutton said, Ballard's message never changed, which grew frustrating. He thought it might be time to listen to some alternative ideas. "Everybody told him he looked funny," Ballard recalls. "Of course, that's what set him apart from the others. But when only Ballard is telling you that your swing is right, you start listening to everyone else—they got him to change. It was the same group of guys, the eight or ten guys who hang around the practice tee on Tour looking for a horse to ride." So Sutton stopped working with Ballard, and coincidentally or not, suffered a temporary slump. Only since the 1994 season, when he began collaborating again with Ballard on a regular basis, has he begun to regain his former brilliant form.

Ballard says that Sutton's story was repeated several times. He has heard from former Tour clients that despite the efficacy of his teaching, they often concealed their association with him. Otherwise, the whispering and snickering campaign would begin. Only J.C. Snead admitted forthrightly why he never told anyone on Tour of his sessions with Ballard: "Hell, I ain't gonna tell anyone I'm working with you 'cause they'll come to see you too, and they'll get better, and that'll take money out of my pocket!"

The Curtis Strange story is a sad one. For nine years, Ballard was Strange's swing guru, and the evidence of Curtis's brilliant record during those years is incontrovertible. But Ballard today feels that he has been undercredited for Strange's success during that time. Although he tries to deal with it, his feelings about Strange unquestionably retain a trace of bitterness.

"A lot of guys have never given me credit," Ballard says. "Curtis Strange worked with me for nine years and never worked with anyone else. I wrote my book in 1979, and Curtis wrote his (*Win and Win Again*) in 1990, about ten years later, after his second Open win. You go take his book and see if it's not almost word-for-word identical. I got extremely upset with Curtis. I helped edit his book, and he never thanked me for it. I got one line in his book, one mention. He didn't mention me at all in his videotape. As far as I'm concerned, it's plagiarism—it's my stuff. Nine goddamn years!"

Ballard is correct that he gets only brief mention in Strange's book. In the introduction, Strange writes, "At the start of the 1980 season my game took a turn for the worse. Soon after that I met and started working with a noted teacher named Jimmy Ballard . . . my game took a turn for the better, and I had a great year." However,

Ballard is credited, along with Strange's father and Chandler Harper, Curtis's first teacher, as one who had a major influence on his career.

As for the plagiarism charge, it might be hard to make it stick. Although Strange does illustrate the basic theory of connection using the same device that Ballard did (throwing a heavy shag bag underhanded, demonstrating how the large muscles must be called into play) and although some of the language is similar, a court of law would no doubt find that there are only so many ways the language can be used to describe a golf swing.

Some of the bitterness may be ascribed to the fact that Strange left Ballard in 1989 to seek the advice of David Leadbetter. Although there is likely a measure of professional jealousy at work, Ballard remains unrepentant in his opinions of Leadbetter. "He ruined Curtis, he ruined Hal, he ruined Sandy Lyle, he ruined Ballesteros, totally ruined 'em!" Ballard maintains. "They were all playing good when they went to him and now they're playing bad." Ballard says that Leadbetter encourages his students to set the angle of their wrist cock early in the swing, which requires a stiff left arm. Disconnection! Ballard also charges that Leadbetter has usurped some of his theories and called them his own. Instead of connection, Leadbetter teaches "linkage." Leadbetter's phrase "the dog wags the tail," Ballard says, is a direct lift from Sam Byrd.

Perhaps Ballard's finest year was 1988, when four adherents of his theories dominated major golf events.

Ballard had spent several weeks that winter with Spain's Seve Ballesteros, who won the British Open that year. He also coached a number of young Swedish golfers, including Christian Harden, who captured the 1988 British Amateur title. Curtis Strange, of course, won his first U.S. Open at The Country Club in Brookline, Massachusetts, that summer in a playoff with Nick Faldo. And another Ballard student, Scotland's Sandy Lyle, had an exceptional spring, capturing the Players' Championship at the TPC at Sawgrass and then the Masters tournament.

A year later, when Curtis Strange defected to the studio of hot guru David Leadbetter, Jimmy Ballard hit something a dry spell. He left Doral intending to move to a swanky new resort called the Ocean Reef Club in Key Largo, Florida. The owners there had promised to build Ballard a state-of-the-art teaching facility, but environmental issues cropped up, suspending the project indefinitely. Ballard is still hopeful that his dream range will be built there some day.

In the meantime he operates his own golf schools, most recently at the Palm Beach Polo & Golf Club in West Palm Beach. But he left that resort in 1995 after a disagreement with the resort's ownership and now plans to team up with old buddy Jim Colbert to open a nationwide chain of Colbert/Ballard Golf Schools.

"The golf school business is changing," Ballard notes wistfully. "When I first got into it, it was nothing to get twenty people to come down to a resort for a week. Today, golfers want more personal attention. And in a golf school with twenty students, they just don't get all of my attention all the time. I see the market changing to more of a personal-trainer type situation. My private lessons are priced at $250 per hour, and I find that people would rather pay that to work with me for an hour than pay $500 for a ten hour school with other people."

Jim Colbert hopes to open thirty to thirty-five golf schools at public courses and driving ranges around the country, primarily in major market areas. Ballard plans to help train the staff for these schools and give lessons from time to time.

Ballard also continues to work with professional clients, including Hal Sutton, who has returned to the fold and snapped out of his slump. Sandy Lyle came back for a week-long recently, too. "He's had bad problems with his thumb for the last two or three years," Ballard says. "I spent fifteen minutes with him and fixed his thumb problems. It was pretty simple!" Like Sutton, Lyle is showing signs of regaining his former brilliance. Ballard also regularly provides his constructive criticism to Sweden's Jesper Parnevik, an up-and-coming star on the world scene.

"I've never gone out on Tour to solicit business," Ballard claims, "And I only work with people who make the commitment to come and spend at least a day with me. I don't think a thirty-minute quick tip on the practice tee does anyone any good. I told a lot of guys, 'Come see me regularly and I'll work with you.' Otherwise it's bullshit. And that made me a lot of enemies out there, too."

There's no question Jimmy Ballard has been knocked around a bit by life. His career has been up, down, and now seems up again, despite celebrity retreats and lack of public acknowledgement of his influence. His mentor, Sam Byrd, used to say that he taught golf through feel and that someday someone would build a machine that would let people feel what he was trying to teach. Ballard thought about that for many years. Finally, in 1988, he sat down with his brother-in-law and a group of orthopedic surgeons from Birmingham and designed an unusual looking swing-trainer machine.

Ballard had carefully measured the movements of the body parts of the great golfers during their swings and found that during a properly connected backswing, the spine shifts six inches to the right. In the throughswing, the spine moves fourteen inches to the left and turns down the line of the swing. He also discovered a third common denominator of the connected swing: the right hip stays dead level as the swing goes through the ball.

So he designed his machine, an odd-looking device with pulleys, straps, and a harness configured to make sure the body moves exactly to those specifications during the swing. "If you get in this machine and you sway, it'll lock up and you can't move. Or if you keep your head still, it'll lock. Or when you get to the downswing, if your right hip goes under, it'll lock. But if you make the proper move, it's smooth as silk." He drags out old videotapes showing first Hal Sutton and then Jim Colbert demonstrating their swings while harnessed in the machine. One golfer complains that his backswing feels shortened (the tapes show it isn't), but both exclaim over the solid strikes that result.

"I can put any beginner in this machine, and they'll hit perfect six-irons in twenty-five minutes," Ballard says boldly. "Probably ten to fifteen minutes."

Unfortunately, he can't prove his point, because he doesn't have a machine to use. Ballard has been swamped in litigation concerning ownership of the device since he built the final prototype in 1989. "I invented it, and these two lawyers want it," he says, shaking his head. "This fight has been going on for five years now. If I can ever get it settled, I can make a million dollars, because this machine will teach feel."

Talking with Jimmy Ballard, one gets the impression that he has been battling life in many ways for many years. Nevertheless, conflict has only strengthened his unwavering belief in his message. "Anybody who ever came to see me in 1965 heard the same thing I teach today," he insists. "I heard from a friend of mine who was warming up for a tournament up in Connecticut that this other guy came up and said, 'You work with Jimmy Ballard, don't you?' And my friend said, 'How do you know?' And the second fellow said, 'I've been working with him since he was at the driving range in Birmingham.' And then he pulled out a battered old notebook, and it had stuff in it from 1962—and it was all the same!

"I haven't changed my teaching ever, and I've only lasted because it's right. I wouldn't be here today otherwise—Lord knows I've never received the credit or the money."

It's tough being the lone rebel against the establishment. Ballard was kicked out of the PGA of America in the early 1960s because he couldn't pass the proficiency test for golf instructors. He refused to endorse mechanics that contradicted his belief about connection. He wouldn't teach players to keep their left arm stiff, their head still, or to turn their shoulders, because he didn't believe in it.

"The PGA turned totally against me because I said they were wrong," he says, defiance still resounding in his voice. "I was the guy who said the world wasn't round—it was square! I nailed a lot of people through the PGA because I set out to teach golf properly by pictures and by looking at what all the great players had in common. Now, they're all teaching what I said all along, and I still don't get credit for it. I know this sounds like sour grapes but it's not. I don't want to come across as a bitter guy, I just want to keep going forward. But this time I'm gonna get the credit for it."

Leafing through a recent issue of *Golf Digest*, he points to a photo spread comparing John Daly to, you guessed it, Babe Ruth—the same Babe Ruth that has been the centerpiece of every golf lesson Jimmy Ballard has given since 1962 and every one Sam Byrd taught in the decades before that. Somewhere up in golf heaven you know old Sam Byrd is grinning like a well-fed hound dog, because Jimmy Ballard sure as hell is.

JIMMY BALLARD

PRACTICE TEE

There are seven common denominators in the connected golf swing.

1. The golfer must create connection at the outset through a braced, connected address position.

2. The golfer must begin the swing by taking the triangle and center (sternum) away together.

3. The golfer must coil the triangle and center behind the ball into the brace of the right leg.

4. The golfer must reverse the club with the right foot and right knee to create the proper position at the top of the swing.

5. The golfer must, after initating the change of direction with the right foot and right knee, immediately release the entire right side and center, ensuring the triangle returns to the original position and squaring the club to the ball at impact.

6. When the club is waist high past the ball, the golfer must have maintained the triangle, with the belt buckle and center facing towards the target.

7. The golfer must complete the swing with the knees, hips, and shoulders level, and the weight entirely on the left side. The straight, balanced finish is proof that connection has been preserved during the swing.

—from "How to Perfect Your Golf Swing," by Jimmy Ballard. 1981, *Golf Digest/Tennis*

Chapter Ten

DAVID LEADBETTER

THE GURU'S GURU

"Uneasy lies the head that wears a crown," wrote Shakespeare.

For the better part of the last decade, David Leadbetter has occupied the throne that belongs to the chief golf guru in the world. His professional students have garnered tournament victories by the bushel, including some of the most prestigious in the world. He has authored instructional books and produced videos that have sold well into the millions of copies. He has established a worldwide network of golf academies bearing his name which command top-dollar bookings. In addition to his busy schedule nurturing the swings of more than two dozen of the top players around the world, he is so sought after to write articles, make golf instructional television appearances, and stage golf clinics and corporate outings, that he has a management group just to take care of the details.

There is no question. David Leadbetter is the king of golf instruction. But despite Shakespeare's maxim, he is far from uneasy. In the rare moments when he has time to reflect, he is thankful for his successes, grateful to those who have helped him along the way, and, truth be told, perhaps a bit regally proud of his noblesse oblige: "the proof of the pudding is in the eating," he says. "I've been very fortunate and I don't deny it. But there are a lot of great teachers in the world who haven't had the success I've had. You make your own luck in this world."

David Leadbetter was born in England but moved soon after with his family to the African nation of Rhodesia, now Zimbabwe. Because of the English colonial influence, growing up in Harare was, except for the warm, dry climate, not unlike a typical English upbringing. As a youngster, Leadbetter enjoyed all the active sports of an English youth: tennis, cricket, rugby, soccer, and golf.

There were a number of notable courses in Zimbabwe, and the country had an active youth golf program that attracted not only the young Leadbetter, but a rather impressive number of golfers who later rated among the best in the world. Nick Price was a boyhood friend of Leadbetter's, and as David progressed upwards in the country's golf circles, he met and competed against Denis Watson, Mark McNulty, Tony Johnstone, and others. "For a very small place, a lot of very good golfers came out of it," he notes with pride.

And David Leadbetter was good. By the time he was sixteen, he carried a handicap of two. Although his parents had encouraged him to pursue his fascination with golf as a youth, they also expected him to enter college and study business. But fate intervened. When the head professional at Leadbetter's home course in Harare announced that he needed an assistant professional, a light bulb flashed in Leadbetter's young brain. "I thought 'hang it!' If I don't make it as a player, I wouldn't mind being a club pro," he says. "I thought it was a good life. I enjoyed the environment of golf and the course, I got to play a lot, and so I decided that I'd see what I could do."

Much to his parents chagrin, Leadbetter dropped out of business school and became a golf professional at seventeen. Within a few years, his game had improved enough for him to compete on the South African Tour for several seasons, although with limited success.

In 1973, the young man decided to visit America. "I thought that if I wasn't going to be successful as a player, I might as well get a decent golf education," he says. Traveling on a three-month tourist visa, he spent most of his time attending teaching seminars sponsored by the PGA of America. He watched Jim Flick and Bill Strausbaugh teach, listened to Gary Wiren talk, and just absorbed the American golf scene.

He returned to Africa intending to relaunch his playing career. He spent several seasons struggling on the European Tour, the South African Tour, and any other pro-fessional event he could qualify for. It was tough sledding, and not just because of the scores he was posting. "It was a difficult period in which to finance oneself," he recalls.

"There were economic sanctions in many countries against those of us from Rhodesia and South Africa, and it was difficult to find money to go and play in Europe. I lived on a shoestring."

Finally, Leadbetter decided that a club job, with its financial security, might be a safer bet for his long-term future. "Looking back now, I think it was a situation where I wanted to be a player but never totally committed myself. Maybe at the back of my mind I felt I didn't quite have it," he admits. "I was probably too much of a perfectionist."

Still, falling back onto golf instruction was not too much of a disappointment for the young man. He had been an avid student of the golf swing since his teen years, collecting magazine articles and swing photos, and talking swing theories with other pros at every opportunity. "In truth, I found teaching to be pretty easy," he said. "I've always found it easy to communicate, which I think is what it's all about, really. I think teaching is 25 percent knowledge and 75 percent communication. You have to be able to communicate to get your message across."

After several years in the late 1970s traveling, teaching, and competing in England and Africa, he was determined to return to the United States and enter full-scale into that golf world he had only briefly tasted during his visit some years earlier. In 1980, Leadbetter's dream finally came true. With the help of teaching pro Phil Ritson, Leadbetter landed a job at a club in Chicago, allowed him the freedom to play competitively on the Florida mini-tours during the winters.

In 1982, he accepted a full-time teaching position at the Grenelefe golf resort in Haines City, Florida, not too far from Orlando. At Grenelefe, Leadbetter immersed himself in teaching, abandoning his playing career once and for all. He both provided private lessons to resort guests and helped run week-long golf school sessions for larger groups of amateurs.

But Leadbetter was destined for bigger things than conducting swing clinics for high-handicap businessmen's groups. He encouraged his old Zimbabwean friend Denis Watson to come to America and try his hand on the U.S. PGA Tour. Watson was Rhodesia's first great golfer, capturing the World Amateur Team title with George Harvey in 1975 and twice representing South Africa in the World Series of Golf.

Watson first joined the PGA Tour in 1981, relying on Leadbetter's teaching as he slowly gained experience with American-style golf. Then, in 1984, Watson had a career year. He garnered three victories that season, including the NEC World Series of Golf at Firestone, which gave him a ten-year Tour-qualifying exemption. He earned more than $400,000 that year, finishing second in Player-of-the-Year voting.

Watson's early success paved the way for another countryman to blaze onto the American scene. Nick Price, born of English parents in South Africa but raised, like Leadbetter, in Zimbabwe, joined the PGA Tour in 1983.

That year he dominated the World Series tournament, solidifying his place on the Tour. In 1991, he began a series of seasons that has established him as one of the most successful players of the modern era. He won two tournaments in 1991, two more in 1992 (including the PGA Championship), then rattled off four wins in 1993 (including three in a row) to capture Player-of-the-Year honors. In 1994, he won the British Open and the PGA Championship, again. It was a stunning display of top-level performance.

But the early successes of the two men rebounded dramatically on the man they shared as golf teacher and friend: David Leadbetter. He suddenly became golf's "hot guru," and Leadbetter's career began to skyrocket.

Still, it wasn't a completely bump-free run to the top for Leadbetter. His next "big-name" client threatened, for a time, to scuttle the entire ship.

Nick Faldo, who Leadbetter had first encountered in African and European tour events during the 1970s, had become the quality of player that Leadbetter had aspired to be, but never quite achieved. Faldo was England's pride and joy during an era that witnessed a huge growth in European golf. Along with Seve Ballesteros of Spain, Bernhard Langer of Germany, Ian Woosnam of Wales, and Sandy Lyle of Scotland, Faldo became one of the premiere players in Europe—and indeed, the world.

But in the late '70s and early '80s, Faldo's game had acquired a propensity to slip when the pressure was on. After a series of less-than-sterling finishes in important tournaments, the pitiless and disappointed British press corps labeled him "Nick Foldo."

"In 1984, Nick was struggling a bit with his game and he felt he needed something to get to the next level," Leadbetter recalls. "He spoke with Nick Price about me, and Nick encouraged him to come see me. Even though I had known him since playing against him in the mid-70s, we had a formal session at the 1984 Million Dollar Challenge tournament in Sun City. I watched him hit and gave him a few thoughts."

That's where matters rested until the 1985 Memorial tournament at Jack Nicklaus's Muirfield Village course in Ohio. "He came to me and said 'I'm really struggling and I want you to throw the book at me. I really want to work at this and I don't care how long it takes.' It was basically let's tear it down and start over."

The two began working intensively, both in England and in Florida. And for nearly two years, while Leadbetter tore his swing apart and put it back together again, Nick Faldo virtually disappeared from the lists of the world's top golfers. And much blame was directed David Leadbetter's way. "His failures were well documented when he was in the doldrums for those two years," Leadbetter recalls. "People were asking 'Who is this guy who's been messing up our national hero?' My name was mud for quite some time."

But in 1987, Nick Faldo won a dramatic and emotional victory at the British Open at Muirfield in Scotland. Nick Foldo was no more, and when Nick Faldo reascended to his place atop the world game, his swing guru soared with him. "When Nick won the Open that year, it was almost as if my career really took off, too," Leadbetter recalls.

Leadbetter's clients have included the likes of Scott Simpson, Larry Mize, Wayne Grady, Bob Tway, David Frost, Mark McNulty, Bob Lohr, Tom Sieckmann, Brian Claar, Mike Hulbert and Larry Rinker. At any given time, he says, there are at least 20 PGA Tour players on the Leadbetter team, plus another dozen or more in Europe, Asia and Australia.

"I think the thing I've found as a teacher is that you learn from the people you teach," Leadbetter says. "I've been fortunate to work with so many of the top players, but really, the only advice I had to give them was what I had learned from working with all the others. In the early years, there was quite a bit of trial and error and guys like Denis Watson and Nick Price, who were my guinea pigs to some extent, helped me more than anything. It was a two-way street: I helped them, and they helped me understand how a player plays."

Although Leadbetter's career has grown along with the fame of his world-class clients, it's his knack for peering at a golfer's swing and quickly discerning where the faults lay that has earned him their attention and admiration. That talent, much like playing ability, is an inherent gift.

"I feel like I have a lot of instinct in teaching," he says. "I can look at a player and say, 'Right, this is what we've gotta do,' and one of my assistants will ask me, 'Why did you do it that way?' And I'll actually have to stop and think about it before I can truly answer him. It's like hitting a bunker shot. You take a world-class player and put him in a bunker and he'll almost have to get in there first and hit the shot before he can describe how he does it. It's a natural thing, and it's a natural thing for me to look at someone and say 'boop, boop, boop . . . that's what I would work on.'"

Leadbetter is a visually oriented person: when evaluating a swing, he "sees" a picture of how the swing *should* look, and then tries to get the student to work towards that mental model. Still, Leadbetter knows not to ignore certain other "clues," such as what the ball is doing. He listens for the "sound of the strike"—the sound of the ball coming off the clubface. He looks to see if the divot the golfer makes is square and of the correct depth. He looks at the trajectory of the ball and the shape of the shot. "Hey, if all that's there, even if something looks a little strange to me, well, obviously the compensations are there to enable that player to hit the shot in that fashion," he says.

His extensive experience has allowed Leadbetter to understand the one common desire of all great players: "They want to control the ball," he says. "That's all they're looking for. What they want in the final result is a sense of 'gee . . . that's it!' The strike felt good, the ball came solidly off the clubface. If they can have control over the ball, then they're going to get near their peak performance.

Assuming, of course, that the other half of their game—putting and 50 yards in—is working as well."

Leadbetter may have started as a pure swing theorist, and certainly still may be, but he likes to think he has taken a more "holistic" approach to golf over time. With both his amateur and professional clients, Leadbetter now stresses physical fitness, proper nutrition, and a positive, esteem-building mental approach to golf, in addition to the tweaks and fixes of the swing itself. "I've always believed that if you can help someone with their golf game, you can help with their attitude, too," he says. "Golf means an awful lot to some people, and it's funny how playing well reflects on one's attitude toward life. I've never seen anyone play great golf and then go home and kick the dog!"

And despite his reputation as a technical teacher and a stern methodologist, Leadbetter insists that swing instruction is just a means to an end, not the end itself. "The only reason you work on your golf swing is so you can get out on the golf course and forget about your golf swing!" he says. "You don't want to work on it just for the sake of working on it. What are you trying to do, create this beautiful, aesthetic looking move? Well, that doesn't get the ball in the hole and the name of the game is 'What did you score?'"

Working with top-level golfers is a different experience than working with amateurs, Leadbetter admits. "People always ask me if it isn't difficult to work with the top players, and to some extent I suppose it is," he says. "But golf isn't like tennis, where a coach has to spent literally all his time with his player. I like to give a player the keys and let them work it out for themselves."

If a Leadbetter client gets totally off track, however, the teacher will make it a point to spend time with him. "There are certain tendencies you have to look for," Leadbetter says. "We all tend to revert back to old habits. A lot of players come to realize that what they think and what they actually do are not one and the same."

In fact, convincing a pro golfer that he is doing something wrong can be the toughest job of a golf instructor. "They'll swear they're doing one thing and feel they're doing it, when in actual fact, they're not. With the advance of video, they can actually see this, and find out the cause-and-effect situation." The key, Leadbetter says, is knowing your own swing and analyzing the situation. In the early stages of his work with a client, Leadbetter will spend most of his tutoring time helping the student understand his swing and how it works. "From then on, it's usually just pieces," he says. "A lot of times now when I'm working with Faldo, we're not doing a whole lot we haven't done in the past."

For the world-class player, David Leadbetter's counsel is mostly a leveling-out process. He calls it putting a player on the scales: as long as they're not popping up on one side or the other, they're fine. "But if there are too many fluctuations up or down, that's when a player is going to be inconsistent," he says. "So what you try to do is find the certain parameters where, as long as they're within them, they're fine."

But for those top clients, Leadbetter serves as much more than golf swing guru. He admits he is also analyst, coach, confidant, cheerleader, psychologist, and more. His job is to coax a player to perform to his potential, and once at that level, to enjoy it as long as possible. Nevertheless, Leadbetter knows that peak performance doesn't last forever.

Nick Price is the prime example. In 1993 and 1994, Price was as dominant a player as the game has ever seen. But in 1995, his performance faltered, at least in comparison to those two all-world years.

"Golf is a game of ups and downs," Leadbetter observes. "And for Nick to follow those last two years with another at such a level would be impossible. I think he was tired in 1995. There is so much pressure put on him, and he's never been one to thrive in the limelight. All the things that have accompanied his great success have made him mentally tired. But I think he's had a chance to recharge his batteries, and I believe we'll see some really great stuff in the next year or two. Whether he can play up to the level of 1993 and '94, I don't know . . . that was almost superhuman!"

Leadbetter disagrees with those who claim Price's blistering face-swing tempo is the cause of his problems. "His fast swing goes with his mannerisms and personality," Leadbetter counters. "In fact, his swing has slowed down over the years. But a golf swing matches one's personality and temperament and Nick is quick and aggressive."

And, Leadbetter claims, if you look at a Price swing in slow motion, there are a lot of good things going on. "All you have to do is listen to his ball strike," he says. "it is really good, really solid. Ben Crenshaw said his strike compares with Hogan. Speed is not the end all and be all. Everybody has his own natural tempo. To tell Nick to slow down would mean diddly."

That kind of swing-matches-the-man philosophy is perhaps a bit unusual in this age of standardization. But Leadbetter is determined to forge his own way in an era of computerization and basic swing models. He acknowledges that today's technology, with its computerized video, helps a teacher store information, make swing comparisons, measure angles precisely, and more. But he also believes that, at its base, teaching is a non-technical art.

"We're dealing with people with feelings and a sensory system," he says. "There's a need for the human element to get a player to play to his potential. The rest is add-ons, perks to help analyze and quicken the learning process. But you have to remember that despite changes in equipment and different role models at different times, the actual physics involved in propelling the golf ball have not changed since the game began! We can make this too complex."

Leadbetter firmly believes that simpler is better. He sees the art of teaching as the ability to sift through information, simplify it, and then communicate the message as clearly as possible.

It is perhaps that drive to simplify and communicate that has made Leadbetter one of the bestselling authors of golf instruction in the game's history. His first book, *The Golf Swing*, published in 1990, sold close to 750,000 copies worldwide. The book is printed in ten languages and is still available only in hardcover. His second book, *Faults and Fixes*, followed in 1993 and has been almost as successful. In it, Leadbetter identifies eighty common swing problems and prescribes solutions for each. In his newest work, 1995's *The Secrets of Great Golf*, he uses the best players in the world, clients and non-clients alike, to illustrate winning swings.

Leadbetter has also produced twelve instructional videos: seven with Nick Faldo, one with Nick Price, and four on his own. He writes regular instruction articles for *Golf Digest* magazine, produces golf-instruction programs for The Golf Channel, and works color and analysis for golf broadcasts on Turner Broadcasting. Of all that, he feels the most influential are the brief, one- to two-minute swing tips he does on TBS telecasts. "Without doubt, those are the things that people love the most," he says. "I've come to realize that most amateurs don't have the time or inclination to spend upwards of an hour or more practicing. So little tips or pieces of information are just right for people to go out and try. We've got a new tape coming that is basically twenty-five of these put together in one place."

Leadbetter has also overseen the development of the worldwide chain of Leadbetter Golf Academies, spread from Japan to Germany, from his home base at the Lake Nona community near Orlando. The development of the academies, however, was largely the result of Leadbetter's association with the powerful management firm, International Management Group. IMG, one of the leading sports management agencies, has long tentacles spread worldwide in the golf industry, and there's no doubt that the company's influence has had a big effect on Leadbetter's career.

But Leadbetter bristles noticeably at the suggestion that his success is the result only of IMG's influence. "I needed management so I could do what I do," he says. "I just like to teach, and I don't like the other side of it, the administrative work. When you're in the public eye, people want you to do certain things, and you have to be careful because there are only so many hours in a day."

Even as he acknowledges that IMG has a reputation for being somewhat ruthless in its business dealings, Leadbetter insists they've been a positive force in his career: managing his affairs, operating the ten worldwide golf academies, and keeping some of the public at bay.

"I mean, I get people calling up all the time offering me any amount of money to get a lesson," he says, shaking his head. "I've been offered $5,000 and $10,000 for a couple hours of my time. It's very flattering, but I tell them I can't teach them anything in just an hour. I suspect much of it is so they can go tell someone they just had a lesson from David Leadbetter."

David Leadbetter, who is already a very rich man, doesn't need to prostitute himself. His priorities are different anyway. "For me, it's a real privilege to be able to mix with these great players, which is the next best thing to doing it yourself. And I've been fortunate over the years to meet heads of countries, kings, and film stars . . . people I'd never had met otherwise. That's the thrill and reward. Sure, the money's nice, but the best thing to me is that I love teaching and I'm in a job where I can help people. It's what I really enjoy: working with an amateur to work things out, taking apart this and that and putting them back together until you find the culprit!"

Leadbetter also tries to maintain a normal home life, which is difficult given his hectic schedule and worldwide globetrotting. He met Kelly Fuiks early in his career when she was a young up-and-coming player on the Florida mini-tours. He helped coach her to victories in the first two U.S. Women's Public Links Championships in 1977 and 1978. She later went on to a career on the LPGA Tour—as Mrs. David Leadbetter. They have three children, the oldest of whom, an eleven-year-old, Leadbetter rates as "a pretty good little player."

If David Leadbetter's head is uneasy wearing his crown, it doesn't show. And he seems to be too busy doing what he does best to spend much time worrying about anyone gaining on him anyway.